SOAP & SOUL

LISA BRONNER

SOAP & SOUL

A PRACTICAL GUIDE TO MINDING YOUR HOME, YOUR BODY, AND YOUR SPIRIT WITH DR. BRONNER'S MAGIC SOAPS

Countryman Press

An Imprint of W. W. Norton & Company
Celebrating a Century of Independent Publishing

For information about permission to reproduce selections from this book, write to
Permissions, Countryman Press, 500 Fifth Avenue, New York, NY 10110

For information about special discounts for bulk purchases, please contact
W. W. Norton Special Sales at specialsales@wwnorton.com or 800-233-4830

Manufacturing by Versa Press
Book design by Allison Chi

Countryman Press
www.countrymanpress.com

An imprint of W. W. Norton & Company, Inc.
500 Fifth Avenue, New York, NY 10110
www.wwnorton.com

978-1-68268-782-6

10 9 8 7 6 5 4 3 2 1

To Pop,
who taught me to be curious and to be kind.

CONTENTS

INTRODUCTION

My middle son was 15 when he moved out of the house. It was earlier than I expected, but considering the year was 2020, not surprising. Seven months into the Covid lockdown with its constant family togetherness, my son, who recharges in his own rhythm of quiet and independence, was done.

One day, he set up our family tent in the backyard, installed an 18-inch-thick air mattress, and personalized it with a comfy chair, a folding table, and a case of Dr Pepper. It was his first home of his own. A drop cord to the house ran a floor lamp, his computer, and speakers. Although he returned indoors for meals and hygiene, he lived in the tent for a month. Because all school was virtual, he also attended classes from the tent—including two hours a day of playing trombone in the band. There's nothing like the dulcet tones of bass brass drifting across the countryside.

While his move was temporary, partial, and a mere five steps from the backdoor, it nonetheless foreshadowed an imminent reality. I could count the months on three hands until our house of five became a house of four, then three, then two. And so I was glad when cold weather brought him back inside.

I understand the craving to have a space of one's own, be it a house, an apartment, or even a tent. A space with the freedom to make all decisions and live with their consequences. To get to say who comes in or out, what gets done and when, what things look like, and how they're taken care of.

My own initial foray into personal home management came later in my life than my son's. For a long time, it didn't go well. Home care was not something at which I instinctively excelled, and there was always something else I'd rather be doing. I've heard of people who simply can't rest until every object and every speck of dirt is in its proper place, who get pleasure from the act of cleaning. That's not me. While I very much like for things to be clean, I wasn't so fond of the process of getting there. For too long, my strategy toward mess and dirt was, "Maybe if I ignore it, it'll go away."

I wasn't much better in my approach to personal care. I was swayed by advertising and packaging and fragrance and texture, and never once thought about product safety. I thought surely somebody somewhere double-checked that sort of thing for me.

Several decades later, I still feel like I owe my college roommates an apology. You'd never have known from me back then that I was connected to the Bronners, the First Family of soap in the natural marketplace. That my family safeguarded an iconic product that's spearheaded clean green living since 1948—a multitasking soap that can single-handedly clean an entire college dorm as well as all the occupants within it.

You wouldn't have known this because I wouldn't have thought it important to tell you, and I certainly didn't act as though I knew more than the next person about soap. At the time, I didn't. Early in my freshman year, my dad shipped me a case of Dr. Bronner's 8-ounce Peppermint Pure-Castile Soap, the company's flagship product. It sat in the hall outside my door for the rest of the year. It took me a long time to realize the worth of the products and the family history that is my legacy.

I am the granddaughter of Emanuel Bronner, who was known to most as Dr. Bronner and the founder of Dr. Bronner's Magic Soaps. His Peppermint Pure-Castile Soap has been recognized for decades by its text-saturated labels and minty zing. The soap that washes everything. The label that says everything.

The company is still run by my immediate family: my two older brothers, David and Mike Bronner, are cosmic engagement officer (CEO) and president, respectively; my mom, Trudy Bronner, is chief financial officer; and my husband, Michael Milam, is chief operations officer. They are joined by many others whose skill and passion power the company today.

Being part of Dr. Bronner's Magic Soaps was not on the radar growing up for any of us—not for my brothers nor me and definitely not for Michael, who had never heard of this quirky soap company before he met me.

David was the first of us to grasp our grandfather's vision, coming to the company in 1997 at the age of 24, shortly after Dr. Bronner died. He had been a mental health counselor in Boston before he felt the tug to come back west. Of the three of us, David most channels our grandfather's undaunted passion, intensity, and tenacity for big causes.

Mike joined in a few years later after teaching English in Japan post-college. With his uncanny ability to develop strong relationships despite language or logistical hurdles, Mike has spearheaded the company's international expansion into over 40 countries.

By 2005, the business was growing by double digits annually, a speed which needs someone relentlessly efficient and data-minded to oversee operations, inventory, and logistics. Enter my husband, Michael (take note—I always call my husband Michael and my brother Mike), who had been a real estate broker in Raleigh, poised to begin an MBA degree with an eye toward commercial development. This left turn prompted our move from North Carolina to California.

My own transition into the company was gradual and unplanned. I had taught high school English for four years before moving into full-time mom mode. Then one day Mike asked if I could answer customer emails. It was a way I could help out, take one of the many hats that he wore, and still be home with the kids. Given that the topics ranged from products to family history to company activism, the task needed someone well-steeped in all aspects. After I'd been handling those for a couple years, Mike suggested I write a blog to answer the most recurring questions en masse and share other healthy tips.

My first response was, "What's a blog?"

Going Green with Lisa Bronner began on March 23, 2010, with a kickoff post about cleaning the microwave with lemons.[1] I went on to analyze popular uses for Dr. Bronner's Pure-Castile Soap and evaluate housecleaning recipes circulating online. This grew to developing official uses and dilutions for the product lines as well as sharing other ways to reduce the burdens in our lives, be they chemical or more intangible.

My work has focused on the micro level of human behavior: the habits and routines of the individual, their daily decisions and habits. Such little everyday practices of home and self-care, when done by a whole population, can have a tremendous impact on the world.

My goal all along has been to connect with people and to help them take the next step from wherever they are toward simpler, more abundant living. To help them remove their burdens in order to live a life that's full of life, of vibrancy, of vitality. I chose the title *Going Green* not because it satisfied the alliterative yearnings of my English teacher's heart—OK, it does that, too—but because it indicates a process. It's the constant effort of leaving things better than we found them, which is how I define "green."

The "-ing" part of "Going" emphasizes that this is continuous. We have started, but we are not finished. Not a single one of us has arrived at the point where we can hang up our hat, kick up our feet, and say, "I've done all that can be done." In this process, we are all at different places. I hope in these pages you find the next steps you might take. I hope amid your circles or even in my online community you can find some fellow travelers to walk beside as you go.

This is a book about taking care of ourselves and our spaces—both tangibly and intangibly. I am ever witnessing how inextricably intertwined our physical, emotional, and spiritual selves are, just as our bodies are with our environments. What is within us connects to what is around us. What elevates the spirit elevates the body. What burdens the body burdens the heart. Soap and soul are tightly bound.

I have become more intentional about setting up my home space wherever I am, however briefly. What my son did by instinct in the tent, I do on purpose because it prepares me for the physical task at hand. When I travel, I unpack my suitcase. Even when I arrive at something as temporary as a meeting, I take a moment to arrange the space around me with a few cues that make it my own. This sets my boundary and says that, in this space, I belong and I am the decision maker.

HOW TO READ THIS BOOK

You've picked up this book perhaps because you want to learn about healthier personal and home care, perhaps because someone gave you a bottle of Dr. Bronner's Pure-Castile Soap and you want to know what to do with it, or perhaps because you've seen some of my tips online and want to have them all compiled in one spot. You're in the right place.

I've arranged this book by rooms of the house because it reflects how I move through my day. I begin by discussing personal care in The Bath and Bedroom because taking care of our bodies needs to come first. Then we can best care for the spaces around us.

Along the way, I share with you my own story of how I came to incorporate healthier practices in my life and home, and to embrace my identity in the Bronner family. I do this to give all the recipes and tips a context, showing how they came to be part of an actual life—mine!

You could settle down in your favorite chair and read through all the narrative sections first, and later, during more lively times of day, put the recipes and tips to use. Perhaps the book will start in your living room and end up in your laundry room.

I added some icons throughout to guide you along.

 LAB COAT MOMENTS: Don your figurative (or not) lab coat for some hands-on chemistry to see the science that's going on behind the scenes.

 ORIGIN STORIES: Learn the when, how, and why behind the creation of various Dr. Bronner's products.

 INGREDIENT SPOTLIGHTS: Get to know the benefits and sourcing stories of certain ingredients used in Dr. Bronner's products.

 ASK LISA: Here I answer some of the most common questions I've received from years of responding to customers.

Over time I adopted the phrase "Green-It-Yourself," or "GIY" for short, to describe the process of making our own simple, low-tox products for home and body. I've used the term GIY for so long now, I forget that I made it up. Where you see "GIY," prepare to get out some measuring tools and a few ingredients. I generally GIY in the kitchen, where these tools are handiest.

To help you further, I have packed my website, LisaBronner.com, with more resources, some fun and some practical. Under the "Book" tab, you will find a list of chapters with instructional videos, PDFs to print, links to products and further reading, and pictures of the many people and situations I mention throughout.

Before I send you off into the rest of this book, what I most want you to know is that I've sought verification for all I share through research and peer-reviewed studies. I've read many hundreds of studies. Whether or not you sludge through my references in the endnotes, know that they are there. As much as I enjoy reading blogs of many sorts, as well as writing my own, these are not what I rely on to substantiate claims.

Furthermore, every recipe and tip in this book is one I have tried and confirmed—except those for which I lacked firsthand experience, such as those intended for beards and mustaches. But I questioned closely those who have used them. These are not ideas I merely read somewhere and thought sounded nifty. Instead, these are methods and techniques I use in my own life.

All in all, you can sum up my message in one word: simplify.

Simplify products. Simplify ingredients. Simplify routines. Simplify spaces. Simplify inputs in all aspects of life. When thus unhindered, the important and the healthful and the beautiful can take full residence in our lives.

WHY LABELS MATTER

Before we get started, I want to have a serious conversation about product labeling, both of personal care and housecleaning products. The time to learn about all this is not while you're standing in the store aisle faced with hundreds of messages bombarding you from every bottle. Instead, educate yourself outside the shopping moment regarding what to look for and avoid. A little education will save you time (because you'll have a good construct in place to parse products quickly), money (because you won't be buying so much through trial and error), and headache (because you'll have the confidence to winnow meaningful messages from mere marketing).

Choosing products for yourself and your house comes down to one reality: no one looks out for you better than you. This means you need to pay attention.

Who Is Looking Out for Consumer Safety?

In the United States, regulation over the content and labeling of personal care and cleaning products is complex and inconsistent. Some aspects are tightly overseen, while others have no oversight at all. This adds up to a confusing landscape for consumers who, without extensive personal research, can't know fully what is in products, how safe they are, or even if what the label says is meaningful.

Part of the problem is that there are so many different government entities who each have jurisdiction over pieces but don't coordinate well with each other.

+ The **Consumer Product Safety Commission (CPSC)** is the default organization that oversees all products sold to consumers unless a product is specifically assigned to another agency. Relevant to the scope of this book is their oversight of cleaning products. Most of the time.

+ The **Environmental Protection Agency (EPA)** oversees any cleaning products that disinfect because disinfectants are considered pesticides. The EPA also sets limits on Volatile Organic Compounds (VOCs) in household cleaners because of their impact on the environment.

+ The **Food and Drug Administration (FDA)** oversees anything marketed to be put on or in the body, including cosmetics and soaps.

+ The **US Department of Agriculture (USDA)**, with its National Organic Program (NOP), oversees the term "organic" as it applies to agricultural products and any products that are made of organic ingredients and can meet the NOP's requirements, including personal care products.

+ The **Fair Trade Commission (FTC)** presides over label claims and specifically regulates certain environmental claims in their Green Guides.

Clear as mud, right?

However, even with—or maybe because of—all of this patchwork oversight, there are massive gaps. In personal care, for example, the FDA operated for over 80 years under the 1938 Food, Drug, and Cosmetic Act, whose 14 sentences about cosmetics feebly attempted to hold the reins on a $100 billion domestic industry.

Prior to recent legislation, the FDA—and the rest of us—could not know which products were on the market, what exactly was in them, or who was making them and where. Manufacturers did not need to report serious adverse events, and the FDA could not issue recalls or restrict ingredients beyond a very short list.

The long-needed federal Modernization of Cosmetics Regulation Act of 2022 (MoCRA) is beginning to change that. In its wake, manufacturers and distributors must register manufacturing facilities, as well as cosmetic products and ingredients; maintain proof of product safety without conducting animal testing (in most cases); report serious adverse health events; test talc for asbestos; disclose to the FDA all flavor and fragrance ingredients; and list any frangrance allergens on labels. In an important stride forward for the safety of salon workers, products sold for salon use must have the same labeling information as those sold direct to consumers. The law also gives the FDA the power to recall and suspend facility registration.

While welcome, this law still leaves work to be done. Since 1938, the FDA has prohibited or restricted only five specific ingredients in cosmetics—bithionol, chloroform, hexachlorophene, methylene chloride, and vinyl chloride—and six compounds—chlorofluorocarbon propellants, halogenated salicylamides, mercury compounds, prohibited cattle materials, sunscreens (now considered drugs), and zirconium-containing complexes. This is despite mountains of evidence regarding other hazardous ingredients, such as formaldehyde, phthalates, parabens, and Poly- and Perflouroalkyl Substances (PFAS)—more on these later.

Because it cannot regulate further, the FDA has resorted to issuing warnings. For example, it has issued a warning on its website that hair-smoothing products often contain formaldehyde, a known carcinogen, which is released into the air as a gas when heated. Heating is often a required step for using hair smoothing products, so the formaldehyde release is inevitable. They've followed a similar warning but not restricting policy for coal-tar hair dyes, which must state on the label that they may cause irritation in some people and blindness if used on eyelashes or eyebrows. All these products are still sold.

In the meantime, in the absence of strong federal oversight, states have been providing their own regulations. As of 2022, California already mandated reporting of fragrance and flavor allergens and made this information public in its searchable Safe Cosmetics Program database.[2]

(Word to the wise: you don't have to live in California to access the database.) Furthermore, California already required ingredient labeling of salon products, and both California and Maryland have laws banning the manufacturing and selling of cosmetics containing 24 hazardous ingredients. More legislation is in the works.

The story with cleaning products isn't much better. Prior to the activation of California's Cleaning Product Right to Know Act in 2020, there was no required listing of ingredients on cleaning products anywhere in the United States. In most of the country, there still isn't, but hopefully this is beginning to shift. New York has now also set a limit on 1,4-dioxane levels—although, illogically, it made them more restrictive for household cleaners (1 ppm) than it did for personal care products (2 ppm) or cosmetics (10 ppm).

Now I hear your question. Does disclosing ingredients mean the products are safer? No. However, disclosure allows those with the knowledge to analyze the lists and educate the public, calling attention to problems and pressuring companies to make improvements in their ingredients. Also, individuals who know their own sensitivities at least have the means to judge for themselves the suitability of a product to their circumstance.

While regulation and transparency may come, so will the development of new ingredients and research that pinpoints new hazards. We will always be playing an ongoing game of whack-a-mole. This is why using fewer and simpler ingredients is wise.

How to Read a Label

What makes reading a product label so tricky is that some of the words on the bottle have very tight definitions and others are complete free-for-alls. This is where the savvy shopper has to do some research.

Regulated Terms
Based on what I've laid out above regarding which agency oversees what, the following words have regulations:

ORGANIC: The USDA controls the USDA organic seal and USDA organic certified claims. Under the NOP, "The USDA organic regulations describe organic agriculture as the application of a set of cultural, biological, and mechanical practices that support the cycling of on-farm resources, promote ecological balance, and conserve biodiversity. These include maintaining or enhancing soil and water quality; conserving wetlands, woodlands, and wildlife; and avoiding use of synthetic fertilizers, sewage sludge, irradiation, and genetic engineering."[3]

Organic standards ensure that certain complex synthetic pesticides, herbicides, and fertilizers are not used on the farms that produce ingredients. In the field, such novel substances make an impact far beyond their purpose, killing nontarget wildlife, creating dead zones in waterways, and ironically *increasing* the resilience of pests and weeds. Organic standards also help keep these chemicals out of and off of the human body, which is ill-equipped to process them.

There are four levels of USDA organic labeling: "100 Percent Organic," "Organic" for 95 to 100 percent organic content, "Made with Organic Ingredients" for 70 to 95 percent organic content, and for less than 70 percent organic content, specific organic ingredients can only be identified as organic in the ingredient list.

However, these do not entirely protect the word "organic." A cosmetics or cleaning product can use the word "organic" on the package so long as it does not claim USDA certification. Another misleading scenario is when the word "organic" is in the brand name only, but not in the product. A product may have certification under a private or foreign standard or not be certified at all. Always look for strong proof of organic claims, such as a known certifier like Oregon Tilth.

BIODEGRADABLE: Overseen by the FTC's Green Guides, a product may be labeled as "biodegradable" as long as there are specifics about how, where, and how long the biodegradation will occur. These specifics make a difference. The example of plastic bags comes to mind. A claim of *soil* biodegradability, which requires the bag be buried in soil, is useless if the bag is probably ending up in the trash (i.e., compacted in a landfill). It won't biodegrade there, and so it is not a meaningful claim.

NONTOXIC: Also overseen by the Green Guides, nontoxic claims "need competent and reliable scientific evidence that the product is safe for both people and the environment." However, they do not go on to define "safe." And given that the FDA only restricts or prohibits a few ingredients, it is a subjective word. Be sure to read the ingredient list for yourself and research anything you don't understand.

COMPOSTABLE: Another FTC regulated term, "compostable" may be used with a qualifier for how and where it can be composted. If it is compostable only in an industrial composting facility, then it won't compost in a home bin. If you don't have access to such a commercial facility, then the claim is irrelevant to you.

Unregulated Terms

The following words have no regulation, which means that they can be used to mean whatever the manufacturer wants them to mean.

NATURAL: "Natural" means nothing. Zip. Zero. Zilch. There might as well be a blank space on the label, and yet it is used ceaselessly on packaging. Nobody wants to define this word. In the words of the FDA: "FDA has not defined the term 'natural' and has not established a regulatory definition for this term in cosmetic labeling." And the FTC: "For sustainable and natural claims, the Commission lacks sufficient evidence on which to base general guidance."

SUSTAINABLE: On its own, "sustainable" is a complete wild card. There is no standard—see the FTC quote above regarding "sustainable and natural." Plus, the word does not address human labor treatment or animal welfare. Look for certifications that monitor ingredient sourcing, soil health, and growing practices, with the incorporation of fair labor and animal treatment and habitat preservation. That is true sustainability.

HYPOALLERGENIC: There is no legal oversight or agreed-upon definition for "hypoallergenic." The term ostensibly means the product doesn't contain allergens, but there is no agreed-upon list of allergens for personal care products, and there is no required verification process for making this claim. I can't say it any better than the FDA: "[Hypoallergenic] means whatever a particular company wants it to mean." Plus, while some ingredients are more known to cause allergies, any ingredient can provoke an allergic reaction among sensitive individuals. Read ingredient lists to look for components to which you might be allergic or sensitive.

NONCOMEDOGENIC: The term intends to communicate that a product does not cause acne (comedones). However, not only is there not a set list of what ingredients cause acne, research on comedogenicity (likeliness to cause acne) has been fraught with disagreement.[4] Furthermore, topical products are not a primary cause of acne. Hormones are the number one culprit, with other research pointing to stress, diet, lifestyle, environment, and genetics. Read ingredient lists if you know a particular ingredient causes problems for you, and explore other causes of acne with your medical advisor. Most importantly, have in place the lifestyle habits of good food, plenty of water, adequate sleep, exercise, and laughter.

ESSENTIAL OILS: The FDA has declined to regulate this term. While I might give a general definition that essential oils are aromatic oils derived from plants, there is no oversight to the term. The term could be used for an ingredient that is very diluted or synthetic.

CRUELTY-FREE: There is no legal oversight to this term, and absent a certification from a reputable certifier, such as Leaping Bunny, it can mean anything or nothing.

GREEN: There is no regulation anywhere for the word "green." It is as meaningless on its own as "natural."

Other Murky Labeling Tactics

XYZ-FREE: Paraben-free, phthalate-free, GMO-free, fragrance-free, dye-free. These are all well and good, but saying what is *not* in the product does not verify what *is* in the product. Still read the ingredient list to find out what is there.

PLANT-BASED: "Plant-based" does not mean vegan. There is no oversight on this word, and even if most or all of the ingredients are indeed plant-based, absent certification there is no guarantee. Some animal-derived

This label is coated with nothing but meaningless messages. But it sure looks good!

ingredients have names that don't seem related to animals, such as car-
mine (a red color derived from the cochineal insect) or royal jelly (from
bees). Many other ingredients have various sources, such as glycerin,
which can come from animal, plant, or synthetic sources. Sometimes the
phrase "natural sources" can even be code for "animal source." Look for
certification that a product is vegan if that is important to you.

GREEN, WHITE, OR MATTE PACKAGING: This is purely a psychological
tug. Green connotes life. White connotes purity. Matte connotes nature-
friendly. Nothing about the outside color of the bottle guarantees what
is inside. Read the ingredients instead.

LEAVES, FLOWERS, FRUITS, SUN, OR ANY IMAGERY FROM NATURE:
This is another emotional pull. It's an attempt to convince the unwary
shopper that the product is blessed by Mother Nature herself. It means
nothing. Look at what's in the bottle.

GREENWASHING

The practice of marketing products as greener, or safer, when they are
not is called greenwashing, and these greenwashed products do more
harm to the advancement of green practices than those that are marketed conventionally. Studies of some products marketed as green reveal
the same hazards as conventional products.[5] This gives a bad rap to the
whole effort. Or worse, consumers gain a false sense of security that these
products are safer and do not exercise the necessary amount of caution
in using or storing them.

To dodge such greenwashing, be sure to keep reading ingredient lists,
and if they are absent or hide in generalizations such as "surfactant" and
"preservative" rather than telling you *which* surfactant and *which* preservative, take that as a red flag.

Certification Verification

Certifications on products, usually presented as a small seal, are a means
of communication between a supplier and a consumer to ensure a claim

is valid and substantiated. Without certification, claims of Organic, Fair Trade, Vegan, Cruelty-Free, Humane, Regenerative Organic, Non-GMO are mere words. A seal from an independent, third-party, external certifier gives these claims meaning. A savvy shopper must learn what seals are from reputable certifiers.

Unfortunately, as with so much, there are folks eager to mislead and distort. They may create what looks like a legitimate certification, but it is not.

FALSE OR MISLEADING CERTIFICATIONS

None of these seals are legitimate certifications from qualified certifiers. They are only pretty artwork, but they sure do look good and probably catch the eyes of distracted shoppers looking for certain phrases.

Here are a few tests to be sure certifications you see on products are sound:

✦ Verify that what looks like a seal on a product represents an actual certification and isn't just artwork made up by the manufacturer. Every certifier has a website. Go look at it.

✦ Verify the seal is the actual authorized certification seal. A marketer could use the wording of a real certification, such as "vegan," but not the correct seal. The seal then is unsubstantiated and meaningless.

✦ Search a certifier's list of certified brands to be sure the brand using the seal is certified and hasn't just pirated the seal. (Yes, the certifier should track down companies who are misusing their seal, but that's another game of whack-a-mole.)

DR. BRONNER'S PRODUCT CERTIFICATIONS: Dr. Bronner's has pursued certifications that are exceptionally rigorous and well established in order to provide the most meaningful assurances to consumers. Most important, these certifications require independent, third-party audits to verify the standards are met. For more information on the standards, please visit the websites of each certification. Here are the certifications you'll find on Dr. Bronner's products and what they mean:

DR. BRONNER'S CERTIFICATIONS

Behind each one of these certifications is an extensive evaluation against strict standards.

USDA ORGANIC: Dr. Bronner's products are certified organic to USDA NOP standards, the same standards consumers trust to certify their organic food. Products with more than 95 percent organic ingredients carry the USDA label on the front, while our Pure-Castile Soaps (over 70 percent organic) carry the "Made with Organic Oils" statement.

OREGON TILTH CERTIFIED ORGANIC (OTCO): Organic certifier Oregon Tilth is a nonprofit that promotes biologically sound and socially equitable agriculture. Oregon Tilth is invested in education, research, and advocacy to grow the organic movement. OTCO is an independent certifier that certifies our products to the USDA NOP organic standard.

REGENERATIVE ORGANIC CERTIFIED®: Regenerative Organic Certified® is a holistic agriculture certification encompassing pasture-based animal welfare, fairness for farmers and workers, and robust requirements for soil health and land management. Our coconut oil, palm oil, and peppermint oil are Regenerative Organic Certified®, and we are working to have all our main ingredients certified in the coming years. Building on organic, this standard combines the best of soil health, fair labor, and animal welfare into a single consumer-facing standard.

FAIR FOR LIFE: Our major ingredients are certified fair trade under the Fair for Life Certification Programme, which verifies that ethical and safe working conditions and fair prices and wages are provided along our entire supply chain. Dr. Bronner's was the first company to establish certified fair trade supply chains for coconut oil and palm oil.

NSF (PERSONAL CARE PRODUCTS CONTAINING ORGANIC INGREDIENTS): Dr. Bronner's All-One Toothpaste is certified to NSF/ANSI 305 standards, meaning it contains at least 70 percent certified organic ingredients but does not meet the NOP food-focused requirements due to processes and methods used in body care production.

LEAPING BUNNY: Dr. Bronner's products and ingredients are never tested on animals, so they qualify for the Leaping Bunny logo through the Coalition for Consumer Information on Cosmetics' (CCIC) Leaping Bunny Program.

VEGAN ACTION: The Certified Vegan Logo certification represents a guarantee that each product is vegan, containing no animal ingredients or animal by-products, using no animal ingredients or by-products in the manufacturing process, and that neither the individual ingredients nor the final product have been tested on animals. All products are certified vegan except the balms, which contain organic beeswax.

B CORP™: Certified B Corps™ are for-profit companies certified by the nonprofit B Lab to meet rigorous standards of social and environmental performance, accountability, and transparency. Since certifying in 2015, every year Dr. Bronner's has been honored as Best for the World in multiple impact areas. In 2022, the most recent year available, Dr. Bronner's earned 206.7 points, far outdistancing the required 80 points to certify.

NON-GMO PROJECT: Dr. Bronner's products do not contain any genetically modified organisms (GMOs). Non-GMO Project verification ensures that our products and ingredients have been evaluated for compliance with the Non-GMO Project Standard.

OK KOSHER: Dr. Bronner's Virgin Coconut Oil is certified kosher by OK Kosher Certification. Final products, along with our manufacturing processes, comply with a strict policy based on kosher food laws, including cleanliness, purity, and quality.

WELCOME TO MY HOME

I'm so glad you've stopped by for this little tour. You are about to enter a single-story ranch house (mine) in rural San Diego County, up in the chaparral-coated hills, where Palomar Mountain looms in the east and the sun glints off the distant Pacific Ocean in the west. It's a long narrow house with a large north-facing front porch.

As you step inside, perhaps you'll say, "This house is so . . ." And I hope the next word is something like "comfortable," "welcoming," or "homey." I'd be disappointed if the adjective you chose was "clean." I don't want you to notice clean. I want you to notice that life is ready to happen here. That is the whole purpose of cleaning. It's not an end in itself. And to be honest, if it's been more than an hour since a vacuuming, there's probably a clump of cat hair visible. This isn't a fussy house. It looks like people live here, with all our quirks and druthers.

In this house in the country, Michael and I have raised our three kids, along with numerous cats and dogs. At dusk the mountains turn purple and the sounds of goats and cows and donkeys and peacocks (none mine) roll across the countryside. Summers are hot and winters are cool, and the misty marine layers of May and June creep up the hillsides each morning, turning the mountaintops to islands in the clouds. Sunrises rival sunsets in their brilliance, and the Milky Way emerges from the inky darkness of new moon nights.

I came to the country having lived all my life in cities, growing up in Los Angeles before college brought me to Durham, North Carolina and then on to teaching in nearby Raleigh. I came to this rural corner of California, pregnant with my second son (the tent-dweller) and have since learned much about wildlife and wildfires, septic systems and solar systems (both kinds), and making-do 30 minutes away from a fully stocked grocery store.

I hope that somewhere on this planet is a place you think of as home, or at least a home base. I hope hearing how I've come to live more fully in my own home and care for myself within it will help you do the same in yours.

Welcome to my home. I'm so glad you stopped by.

CHAPTER 1

THE BATH AND BEDROOM

Never let a good crisis go to waste.
—MICHAEL MILAM

Bedrooms bookend our days. Here our days begin and end. There's a natural rhythm to our departure and return to this room. Whether the day holds triumph or disaster or merely the everyday effort of doing the best we can, the bedroom bounds it all.

In my bedroom, which is a deep serene blue, I wake up each morning and sometimes I reflect, "Once I leave this bed, I will not stop moving until I return to it again."

Between those bookends sometimes something extraordinary occurs.

It was dusk one unremarkable day. I hadn't turned on many lights. The dimness matched my mood. I was holding my three-month-old son. He battled infant acid reflux and was most comfortable when I was holding him, which I was happy to do, but still . . .

I was hosting my own little pity party. I felt weighed down by more than my son on my hip. My spirit was heavy with thoughts of how hard simple things seemed to be, from taking a shower to getting enough sleep, let alone taking care of the spaces around me. I just wanted things to be easier.

In that moment what I wanted to do was not exotic. I just wanted to tidy my room. By myself. With both my hands. If I had both my hands available, it would be so much easier and the task would get done so much faster.

With a sigh and my one free hand, I picked up a book—clutter in my house is usually made up of books—from the dresser, trudged over to the shelf, and put it away. Then I paused. I looked at the bookshelf. I looked at my hand. I looked back at the out-of-place spot the book had been, now empty. And the light dawned.

I had one free hand. That hadn't occurred to me before. I'd been too focused on my unavailable hand. I didn't have two free hands, but I had more than none. I could use that one free hand to make progress, albeit slower, but progress nonetheless. Back and forth I went between that cluttered dresser and the items' homes. Slowly the dresser got cleared, and I marveled at the progress. It was eye-opening and instructive.

It was in that moment that I learned to relinquish the ideal in exchange for the possible. To focus on what I could do instead of what I couldn't. Value progress, not perfection.

Oh, I know this isn't an original thought, but this was the day it came home to me. It broke a paralysis of perfectionism. I couldn't do everything exactly the way I wanted to, but I could do something. And some days I could do more than others so long as I got started.

This lesson of doing what I can, even if not ideal, stuck with me. When the paralysis creeps close, I can mutter to myself, "Do something, not nothing. Take the next step." Learning to take that next step, whatever it may be, has kept me moving when things are hard.

This is always my advice to people who are just starting their green journey if they have the luxury of time. Take it one step at a time, one change at a time, so that you don't overwhelm yourself. There is a lot to learn in making the transition to green, from understanding labels to figuring out replacements and adapting to new routines while maintaining schedules and budgets and energy. Start with one product to change—either an easy one or one that really bothers you—and fix that one. Figure out what would be a better, safer option. Once that is in place, move on to another product. Before you know it, you'll get them all swapped out.

However, another all-too-common prompting to go green is a crisis, such as a health diagnosis or perhaps an allergy, when you may need to make the switch all at once. If this is the case, take a deep breath. You'll be OK. It may be a steep climb at first, but you will get there. What you will find, with both body care and home care, is that a few versatile products can replace 10 of the products you just had to ditch. I'll walk alongside you.

Returning to the idea of bedrooms as bookends, bear in mind that the purpose of bookends is to provide support. Sleep is the primary support, but here's another small way bedrooms can support our days: when you wake up in the morning, before you go far, maybe even before your feet hit the floor, take a moment to fill the spirit before you start to expend yourself into your day. Doing so will mean you have more to give. Read something inspirational, say a prayer, meditate, or breathe a few deep intentional breaths. Peek out the window and see the sunrise. Anything that stills the body and checks in with a larger perspective.

After this spiritual "wake up and fill up" comes the daily transition into productivity. After years of stumbling about, fighting the same early morning battles against inertia and indecision, I finally landed on four tasks that are the linchpins to get my day moving. I call these my First Four. They need doing every morning, so there's no decision. The answer is yes. They are:

+ Dress ready for the day.
+ Make my bed.
+ Empty the kitchen sink.
+ Start a load of laundry.

The external impacts the internal. With these four, my body is ready, my spaces are ready for whatever comes next. Whatever else my day holds, these First Four have built the momentum to tackle it. I've already overcome a few forces of chaos and am ready for more. I once heard

Admiral William H. McRaven, former Navy SEAL, tell a graduating class at the University of Texas at Austin, "If you want to change the world, start off by making your bed." Anything can happen after that. And even if the rest of the day spirals off course, I can look at the Four and say, "I did that."

Returning to the bedroom at the day's end, we've reached the other bookend. It's time to write a Tah-Dah list. Tah-Dahs redeem days that ran amok and bolster days that appear to have fallen flat, as books tend to do when the bookend isn't in place.

Tah-Dah lists are drastically different from to-do lists. To-do lists are lists we make at the beginning of the day, when we write down everything we intend to get done. And then at the end of the day, we may look at that to-do list and realize we did none of that. It's very discouraging.

Tah-Dah lists are far superior. In them I record everything I accomplished in that day, big and small, whether I had intended to or not. This is how to incorporate, and even justify, all that unplanned stuff that derailed the to-do list. It transforms the unexpected into an accomplishment. The list starts with the First Four: Made bed. Tidied kitchen. Washed a load. Dressed. Then maybe: Mopped the floor. Read to my son. Washed the dog. Paid a bill. Handled that unexpected phone call. Dealt with that bathroom disaster. Cleaned up after a sick dog. Washed the dog again.

And here's the magic: unlike on a to-do list, everything on a Tah-Dah list is already done.

We cannot always control what our days contain, but as much as possible, we can set ourselves up for success by starting and ending our days with habits that strengthen.

My journey in understanding body care has also been a journey in understanding myself. When Michael and I moved to California in 2005, the crisis came home. In moving to an unfamiliar place, all my cushions and crutches and comfortable distractions got left behind, and without their smoke screen, I found I was not the person I thought I was.

I had gotten into the habit of shirking work and tedious to-dos. I had yet to learn to open my days with the First Four and to close them with Ta-Dah lists. When any task got tough or annoying, I flitted to the next thing, leaving a trail of the undone. I hated learning that about myself. The result was that I wasn't caring for myself well, my house was messy, I ate oddly, I slept poorly, I was constantly frustrated because of all that, and in desperation I grabbed at whatever products promised ease and respite, whether for my body or for my home. I was not in control of myself or my spaces.

What I needed was resilience to stick to hard tasks and honesty to see myself and my situation clearly. I found I was burdened by a surfeit of identities—of people I had been and wanted to be. By this point in my life, I had already had several different adult identities—student, teacher, wife, freelancer, parent, gardener, painter—and I needed to close out some of these identities that were no longer active. Then I could fully embrace those that were still relevant.

This was not a mere internal identity issue. All these various identities were cluttering up my drawers and closets with unused equipment, weighing down my house, and getting in the way of accessing what I needed for today. These old identities needed to go!

This idea of naming identities, and relegating them to the past, gave me a strong framework to apply to the objects in my house. "Is this item part of who I am today, or will it be part of my certain future?" If not, out it went. This also helped me when shopping. "Does this item fit who I am right now or into the clear direction I am going?"

As I cleared out the non-me stuff, I felt my spirit settle and expand more fully into who I was in the moment, no longer pressed by the crowd of outdated or never-to-be identities. There's nothing wrong with memories, and there's nothing wrong with dreams. But when "what was" and "what might be" block me from accessing "what is" right now, I miss out on fully living in the present.

Sticking to this task of introspection and examination of who I was and was not gave me grounding, strength, and freedom.

Once I was no longer pulled in so many directions, I felt less frenzied and desperate in the ways I took care of myself. When I turned to look at my personal care products, I had the tranquility to examine them carefully instead of frantically bouncing from one to the next in hopes that they'd fix me.

Instead of making my decisions based on advertising, packaging, or sales, I began to look at ingredients and formulations. This is where I came to the truth I oft repeat: chemistry matters. It matters infinitely more what is *in* the bottle than what is *on* the bottle.

As I studied more and more about ingredients, I kept coming up against the same conclusion: dial it back. Reduce the number of products. Reduce the number of ingredients. Simplify, simplify, simplify.

And more important than anything else I can possibly say about products and skin care, remember this: healthy skin and body care begins with lifestyle. If you can't read any further than this point right here, you'll still have gained the most essential takeaway: health and beauty don't come primarily from a bottle.

Before you invest money, time, or attention on a new skin care regimen, make sure these are in place:

+ Eat nutritious whole foods.
+ Drink plenty of water.
+ Get 7–9 hours of sleep each night.
+ Exercise regularly.
+ Relax.

There is no product of any sort that can compensate for the lack of these five life habits.

And the fastest, cheapest, most effective, and most deeply scientifically proven way to look more attractive, younger, even thinner?[6] Smile.

Once those are in place, the next most important skin care fundamental is to dial back the number of products and dial back the number of ingredients in the products. This gives you less to keep track of, gives your budget less to spend on, gives your cabinets less to store, and most importantly, gives your body less to grapple with. With fewer ingredients, there are fewer possibilities your body will react to one, and if it does, it's easier to pinpoint which one is the problem. With simpler ingredients, you're giving the body what it can understand and process.

My own exercise in product and ingredient simplification continued until I ended up with a shower holding all of two products and a bathroom cabinet with plenty of white space. At the center of it all was one very simple soap that happened to be my family's legacy.

GOING GREEN WITH OUR BODY CARE

Another bookend to our days is our body care. While there might be a midday touch-up—a quick brush of the hair or teeth—most of our personal care is done in the morning and in the evening. In fact, our body care can serve as a segue out of and back into our times of rest, providing cues both to wake up and wind down.

The focus here is on how we care for our body in all its life stages, from infancy into adulthood. When you hear of the idea of chemical exposure, perhaps you think of billowing smokestacks or industrial sewage discharging into rivers. While those are real, the chronic daily chemical exposure most of us face is in the products we put on our bodies. Between our cleansers, moisturizers, skin treatments, powders, deodorants, perfumes, colognes, and makeup, we apply, on average, 13 products daily to our bodies, with 169 unique ingredients. Since the burden is on the consumer to track and ensure their safety, that adds up to a lot of work. Let's start by looking at what some of these ingredients are and then examine safe alternatives for any hazards.

Before I jump into the recipes and tips, I want you to take a moment to see some of the bigger picture behind body care and the industry that supports it.

Points to Remember Regarding Body Care

1. The skin is permeable. Our skin is a complex paradox that provides both a barrier to protect what's inside the body and a sponge that allows things through.

2. "All-day" products merit greater scrutiny than "wash-off" products. The longer a product is in contact with the skin, the greater the possibility for absorption. Leave-on products are lotions, deodorant, sunscreen, makeup, and perfume/cologne. Wash-off products are soaps, shampoos, conditioners, shave gels. I mention this as a matter of prioritizing if you're wondering where to start making changes first.

3. The "cocktail effect" is more important than ingredients in isolation. We almost always apply ingredients in combinations. An ingredient that may be safe on its own may not be safe in certain combinations. Because we tend to apply products on top of each other—say, perfume or cologne on top of sunscreen on top of lotion—we need to consider not only the combination of ingredients within one product but also the combination of ingredients across all of the products we apply.

4. Products marketed to people of color consistently contain more hazards in the form of endocrine disruptors, asthmagens, and carcinogens, as well as ingredients more likely to cause hair loss. Hair relaxers are particularly problematic, even though many have labeling messages implying they are safer. Hair colorants score even worse.

Hazardous Ingredients to Avoid in Your Personal Care Products

The only way to know if there are hazards lurking in the products in your bathroom cabinet is to read ingredient lists. That may sound daunting, but there's no way around it. Eventually, when you've been doing it for a while, you'll skim right through them. Your eyes will flow over words like mesoisothiazolinone and diethanolamine, and you'll feel powerful—like you know some secret language. Which you will! For the curious, there is much more detailed information on each of these ingredients in the Appendix (see page 237).

+ Quaternary ammonium compounds (quats) and ureas
    + Quaternium-15
    + Diazolidinyl urea
    + DMDM hydantoin
    + Imidazolidinyl urea
    + 2-bromo-2-nitropropane-1,3-diol (bronopol)
+ Isothiazolinones
    + Mesoisothiazolinone
    + Methylchloroisothiazolinone
+ Certain Parabens
    + Propylparaben
    + Butylparaben
+ Retinyl palmitate
+ Glycols
    + Polyethylene glycol (PEG)
    + Propylene glycol
+ Ethoxylated compounds
    + The suffix -eth or -oxynol
    + Polyethylene
    + PEG
    + Polyoxyethylene
    + Polysorbate

continues

+ Poly- and Perflouroalkyl Substances (PFAS)
+ Ethanolamines
  + Diethanolamine (DEA)

And to a lesser extent:

+ Triethanolamine (TEA)
+ Monoethanolamine (MEA)

AND THEN THERE'S "FRAGRANCE": Unqualified, the word "fragrance" in ingredient lists should be avoided if no further transparency is available, especially for people experiencing sensitivities. The word "fragrance" is not a single ingredient, but a blend of ingredients that don't have to be disclosed. The term can conceal any of over 3,000 potential ingredients. Fragrances and preservatives are the most common source of allergic contact dermatitis in cosmetics. Of the 40 common allergens listed by the FDA, 35 are fragrance or preservative compounds.[7] Even products marketed as "unscented" may contain masking fragrances to cover the scent of other ingredients.

SUMMING IT UP

Hopefully at some point this list will be outdated because, either through consumer pressure or regulation, these ingredients will no longer be used. Until that happens, familiarize yourself with ingredients that nourish and build, lead a healthy lifestyle, and simplify your products and ingredients.

WHAT IS CASTILE SOAP AND HOW IS DR. BRONNER'S PURE-CASTILE DIFFERENT?

While soap has been around for millennia, early soaps were made from animal fats, such as tallow (from cattle) and lanolin (from sheep). Castile soap is one of the earliest vegetable oil soaps, made from olive oil from the Castile region of Spain. In more recent times, although castile soap still features olive oil, the term has come to include additional vegetable oils.

"Castile" is not a regulated term, however, so a product can be called castile and contain no olive oil whatsoever or may even contain a synthetic detergent like Polysorbate 20, which brings us back to the importance of reading ingredient lists. I'll tell you more about soaps versus detergents in The Cleaning Cabinet chapter on page 79.

What sets Dr. Bronner's Pure-Castile Soap apart from other castile soaps is that it contains no artificial fragrances, detergents, preservatives, or dyes. Instead, tocopherols (vitamin E) are added for longevity, and the products are scented only with pure essential oils. A final contributor to our soap's smooth afterfeel is the retained glycerin. Glycerin is a natural by-product of the soapmaking reaction. Some soap makers drain it off and sell it as a side product, but leaving it in makes the soap more soothing to the skin.

I use castile soap, specifically Dr. Bronner's, throughout this book and my life because of its extreme simplicity. It lacks the hazards I've mentioned. It leaves no residues on skin or on household surfaces, which will be relevant in later chapters. It contains nothing extra—no fillers, no dyes, no synthetic foaming agents. It is pure soap made with ingredients you can understand without resorting to a database. Dr. Bronner's Pure-Castile also is as concentrated as it can possibly be: the liquid has just enough water to keep it liquid. In fact, if you accidentally leave a bottle uncapped, you'll notice that the soap very soon starts to solidify as the water content evaporates.

INGREDIENT SPOTLIGHT
Hempseed Oil

One of the only ways the formulation for Dr. Bronner's Pure-Castile Soap has altered since my grandfather's day was the addition of hempseed oil in 2000 to work in tandem with the jojoba oil to make a skin health–promoting powerhouse.

Hempseed oil is an exceptional oil, pressed from the seeds of the *Cannabis sativa* plant. It differs from cannabidiol (CBD) oil, which comes from the leaves and flowers. It is the only plant source of vitamin D and contains the nutritionally optimal 3:1 ratio of omega-6 to omega-3 fatty acids in the forms of linoleic and alpha-linolenic acids, respectively. The one downside to this oil is that you can't cook with it. It oxidizes when heated beyond 200°F (93.3°C) or exposed to light, so it's only good as a cold oil and must be stored in the fridge when in pure form. Our body care formulations that contain hempseed oil, however, are shelf stable.

For topical applications, no plant source comes closer to the fatty acid profile naturally occurring in human skin than hempseed oil. The most abundant polyunsaturated fatty acid in our outer layer of skin is linoleic acid, the same omega-6 mentioned above, which makes up roughly 55 percent of hempseed oil.

Oils with a high linoleic to oleic acid ratio have better ability to repair skin and improve skin barrier function.[8] Hempseed oil's ratio is an impressive 6:1.[9] Various studies have concluded it increases skin moisture without clogging pores, shows antibacterial properties, slows aging, and reduces inflammation.[10] It's like it's showing off.

Some wonder if using topical hemp products may trigger a false positive for *Cannabis sativa*'s psychoactive component, tetrahydrocannabinol (THC). However, studies show that even concentrated THC applied to skin does not register in blood or urine.[11] Further, Dr. Bronner's complies with US law and verifies that our hempseed oil contains less than 10 ppm THC, far below what could trigger a false positive.

Then there's the caliber of the raw materials in Dr. Bronner's products. Whenever possible, they are organic, fair trade, non-GMO, even Regenerative Organic Certified®.

I formulated the recipes throughout this book that call for castile soap using Dr. Bronner's. If you want to try out another brand, be sure to read the ingredient list and take note of the undiluted soap concentration by conducting the following experiment. If another castile soap is half as concentrated as Dr. Bronner's, you'll need to use twice as much in each recipe.

LAB COAT MOMENT
Comparing Concentration

Pour 1 tablespoon (15 ml) of Dr. Bronner's Pure-Castile Soap and another castile brand into side-by-side, identical small glasses. Shot glasses would be perfect. Let them sit uncovered for several days while the water content evaporates. You might need to stir them with a toothpick occasionally to push aside the solidified soap at the top and allow more of the liquid beneath to surface. Once the water has evaporated, what is left behind is the soap content. Compare the two amounts and see which glass contained more soap content and which contained more water per total volume. A higher concentration of soap means you need to use less each time, and your bottle lasts much longer. Money saved!

WHAT'S THE DIFFERENCE BETWEEN DR. BRONNER'S SOAP TYPES?

While my grandfather started the company with the Pure-Castile Liquid Soap, new soaps have been added to the line-up: Pure-Castile Bar Soap, Organic Sugar Soap, and Organic Shaving Soap. The Pure-Castile Liquid Soap is the simplest of the Dr. Bronner's soaps. It contains only a blend of five oils that have been saponified—that is, turned into soap using potassium hydroxide—and a few extra ingredients for mildness (citric acid to balance the pH), longevity (tocopherols), and scent. The only addition to the scented soaps are the essential oils. The soap base is the same, except the Baby Unscented, which contains no essential oils and twice the amount of olive oil in ratio.

The Pure-Castile Bar Soap mirrors the ingredients of the Liquid, but the oils are treated differently. Only three of the oils are saponified, with the hempseed and jojoba oils added after saponification to "superfat" the soap, which makes it more moisturizing. The saponifying agent in the bar is sodium hydroxide instead of potassium hydroxide, but in both cases the hydroxides are completely consumed in the reaction, with none remaining in the final product. Other differences further increase the hardness of the bar: a lower concentration of essential oils and the addition of sea salt. The bottom line for performance is that the Pure-Castile Bar Soap is slightly more moisturizing but less scented than the Pure-Castile Liquid Soap.

The Organic Sugar Soap has a base of the Pure-Castile Liquid Soap but receives a boost of moisture and mildness from organic white grape juice, organic sucrose, and organic shikakai powder, which I'll explain in greater detail in a moment. The Organic Shaving Soap, which is the Organic Sugar Soap with a thicker concentration of these additions, takes the moisture up even further.

ORIGIN STORY:
Dr. Bronner's Organic Sugar Soap

For years, we received pleas from customers for a soap that worked in a pump. The Pure-Castile Liquid Soap has never worked well in a standard soap pump because it is so concentrated that as soon as any of the water content evaporates, the soap starts to solidify. When it solidifies inside a pump, it creates a jet of soap that shoots sideways or up, dousing a wall, a shirt, or a face.

David spearheaded this project and at the same time decided to address several other customer requests for a soap that was more moisturizing for dry skin and hair, and was certified USDA Organic. (For a product to qualify for the USDA Organic logo, it must be made with 95 percent organic materials. However, for the Pure-Castile Soap to be properly made, the amount of necessary mineral alkali drops the percentage of organic ingredients below that 95 percent threshold.)

So starting with Pure-Castile base, David replaced the water that liquified the soap with organic white grape juice. This, along with the addition of organic sucrose, boosted the sugar content of the soap. Sugar is a natural humectant, which means it draws moisture into the skin. Then he added organic shikakai powder (see page 44) to increase the mildness and softening ability of the soap. Thus was born in 2007 the Organic Sugar Soap: extra nourishing for skin and hair, certified USDA Organic, and workable in a standard pump. We were so excited about the addition of the shikakai powder that we originally called this Organic Shikakai Soap, but after several years of tongue-twisting and sometimes embarrassing mispronunciations, we decided to highlight another of the excellent ingredients and simplified it to Organic Sugar Soap.

INGREDIENT SPOTLIGHT
Shikakai Powder

The word *shikakai* literally translates to "hair fruit" or "fruit for hair." While not abundant in Western hair and skin care products, shikakai powder has been used in traditional Indian hair and body care products for millennia.

Shikakai comes from the *Acacia concinna*, a shrub-like tree that grows in the tropical rainforests of southern Asia. As part of the legume family, it grows long-ridged fruit that look like dark brown pea pods. When dry, these pods are ground into a fine powder similar in color and texture to ground cinnamon. This is what we call shikakai, and it is amazingly good at cleansing and nourishing skin and hair.[12]

Shikakai softens and moisturizes skin, which always gives our skin a more youthful appearance. It also is naturally high in vitamins A, E, and K—all of which help promote and maintain healthy skin—and vitamin C, a naturally occurring antioxidant that brightens skin.

Shikakai does something pretty unique: it gives true soap a near-neutral pH. Soap is always alkaline (the Pure-Castile Soap sits at a mild 9.3 ± 0.3), and attempting to neutralize the pH down to 7 will break down the soap molecule. However, shikakai saponins have a naturally low pH between 4.5 and 5.5. When added to soap, they lower the overall pH of the soap down to a super mild $8.5 \pm .5$ without destroying the soap molecule. They are able to do this because the shikakai saponins are anionic surfactants (not charged), whereas the soap is an ionic surfactant (charged).

RECIPES AND HOW-TOS

This is where the fun starts! Let's walk through personal care routines for adults, children, and even infants, and find how easy it is to replace conventional products with a few simple, nontoxic ingredients.

FOAMING HAND SOAP

This is one of the two dilutions using castile soap I want you to put down this book and go make right now. The other is the GIY All-Purpose Cleaning Spray (page 91), which we'll get to in The Cleaning Cabinet. As I mentioned above, the Pure-Castile Soap does not work well in a standard pump, but it works gorgeously in a foaming pump. Foaming pumps have a small chamber that forces air into the liquid solution. It's a great way to keep kids (or absent-minded adults) from using too much soap. And foam is fun.

I use all sorts of foaming pump dispensers—one at every sink from the bathroom to the kitchen. Mason jars with special tops; plastic bottles with suction cup bottoms; and a touchless, rechargeable dispenser by my kitchen sink.

I use the foam for washing my hands, my face, my night guard, my makeup brushes, and in the kitchen for washing a piece of fruit, a single dish, or on a washcloth to wash a counter.

1 part Pure-Castile Soap
3 parts water

HOW TO:

1. In your foaming pump, combine the soap and water. If you have a 1-cup pump, this would be ¼ cup Pure-Castile Soap and ¾ cup water. Distilled, reverse-osmosis, or softened water will make a clearer solution, but any water is fine. Cloudiness in the solution is a sign of water

hardness, discussed on page 99, and is harmless. It will settle at the bottom of the jar. It is not the soap and does not need to be mixed back in.

2. Swirl to mix.

Body Washing

Body washing is the primary use for the Pure-Castile Soap and what I use from head to toe. Details are coming, but I can assure it is lovely to have just one product in the shower for hair, face, and body. No fuss. Whether you squirt a little Pure-Castile Liquid Soap into a washcloth or dilute it in a foaming pump, or perhaps you prefer to lather the bar in your hands or use a pump of the more moisturizing Organic Sugar Soap, you'll be cleansing your body in the simplest, healthiest way possible.

WIPE-OFF CASTILE BODY WASH SPRAY

When my daughter was 10, she broke her leg skimboarding and was casted from her hip to her toe. The cast was huge and green. We called it her frog leg. She wasn't amused. She was even less amused at the prospect of not taking a shower for eight weeks.

When running water isn't an option—due to a disability, illness, a large cast or bandage, or when hiking or camping—a wipe-off soap spray is a great way to stay clean.

1½ teaspoons (7.5 ml) Pure-Castile Soap
1 cup (240 ml) water

HOW TO:

1. Combine in a spray bottle. To use, spray lightly on skin, then wipe with a wet (not dripping) cloth. Dry skin.

Face Washing

When I say I wash my whole self, head to toe, with Pure-Castile Soap, I do mean it all. Face and hair, too. I've tried many other facial products. I've used the beautifully marketed products. I've used the special-order products. I've even used prescriptions. It wasn't until I tried our Tea Tree Pure-Castile Soap that I found what I was looking for: skin that was clear and well-balanced and resilient.

PURE-CASTILE SOAP FACE WASH

Skin needs at least two weeks to adjust to a new regimen. Some derma-tologists say 30 days. You may notice increased breakouts, increased redness, increased tightness during this time. This can be part of the skin's purging, deeply cleaning pores of sebum and dead skin cell accumulation. Sometimes as they leave the pores, they get stuck at the opening, causing a temporary clog. This is why the adjustment period is necessary.

Keep skin nourished with a simple moisturizer, sunscreen during the day, and healthy lifestyle habits. If you find your skin still feels tight, try the Organic Sugar Soap with its extra softening and nourishing ingredients.

HOW TO:

1. Lather 2–3 drops of the Pure-Castile Liquid Soap in the hands, work up a good lather from the Pure-Castile Bar, or use two squirts from the foaming pump dispenser.

2. Massage into the skin in circular motions with the fingertips for 20 seconds. Do not use a rough cloth or scrubbing agent. This is too intense for facial skin.

3. Rinse well with warm, not hot, water. Blot skin dry.

NOTE: True soap is never tear-free, which I'll explain on page 71, so keep the eyes closed.

REMOVING MAKEUP

Dr. Bronner's Pure-Castile Soap lifts sunscreen and even the heaviest concealer and foundation. Washing with it at the end of the day makes my skin feel brand new.

However, for makeup close to the eyes, especially waterproof eyeliner and mascara, dissolve it with pure Dr. Bronner's Virgin Coconut Oil instead. No fancy multi-ingredient makeup remover—just one simple oil. Coconut oil works because many mascaras and eye liners, especially if they're waterproof, are oil- or wax-based. Oil dissolves oil. Also, coconut oil does not have a pH and so will not irritate the eyes.

I use this after I've washed my face, and I leave the residual coconut oil as a moisturizer. However, you could do this before you wash the rest of your face to wash off the residual coconut oil.

HOW TO:

1. With the tip of the ring finger, gently massage coconut oil into the liner and mascara.

2. Wipe away with a washable/reusable cotton pad, a soft tissue, or a cotton ball.

CLEANING MAKEUP BRUSHES

Makeup brushes must be cleaned regularly to remove the buildup of makeup, oils, and bacteria. If it's been a while since you cleaned yours, the first time may startle you and convince you to clean them more often.

HOW TO:

1. Wet the makeup brush well.

2. Apply a drop or two of the Pure-Castile Liquid Soap or one pump of foaming soap to the bristles. Alternatively, run the brush across the Pure-Castile Bar Soap.

3. Massage throughout the bristles. Add more soap for larger or more caked brushes.

4. Fill a bowl with clean water and rinse the bristles. If the water gets too murky, empty it and refill.

5. Gently blot the bristles with a clean towel and allow to air dry completely.

6. Fluff the bristles once dry.

Hair Washing

Now that we've covered cleansing skin, let's move on to the topic of hair. I consider this taking GIY to the next level. I cannot tell you how freeing it is to wash my whole self with one product. It's simple and it leaves my shower delightfully uncluttered.

The tricky thing about hair recommendations is that there is so much variety in hair types and preferences. I won't be able to tell you exactly what will work best for you and the look you want. What one person calls "sleek," another calls "flat." What one person calls "full of body," another calls "wild and out of control." You must figure out what works best for you, but I'll get you started with what has worked for me.

The fundamental difference between shampoo and soap is that shampoo is a detergent. Don't jump down the "detergents are bad" rabbit hole because they're not all bad, and not all soaps would be good for hair. However, many of the problematic ingredients I mention above abound in conventional shampoos, which is a key reason to find an alternative.

A true soap is always alkaline. Always. There is no way to have a soap that is not alkaline. I'm talking about pH here, that concept you studied in school when you reacted vinegar (acid) and baking soda (alkali). Detergents have more flexibility and are able to be acidic.

The outermost layer of hair strands, called the cuticle, is a mass of overlapping cells like scales. In the presence of an alkali, such as a true soap, these scales stand up. If left this way, hair feels tacky. The strands catch on each other, tangling readily, and do not reflect light, making the hair appear dull. Acids smooth these scales, which means that, when washing with soap, an acidic rinse is needed to rebalance the pH.

While I usually use the Pure-Castile Liquid Soap to wash my hair, I switch to the Organic Sugar Soap during drier months and the Organic Shaving Soap during the driest times of all. The Pure-Castile Bar Soap can work for me, but it takes a while to work it through my long hair, and I'm impatient. Michael, however, uses the Pure-Castile Bar Soap and, with his short, stiff hair, can wash his hair with soap and go. No conditioning rinse. Lucky duck. I need the conditioning rinse to smooth my long, fine hair.

Fortunately, most of us are accustomed to a two-step hair regimen, so the idea of a conditioning rinse isn't too troublesome. For the acidic rinse, there are three ready options: lemon juice, apple cider vinegar, or Dr. Bronner's Citrus Organic Hair Rinse, which has a base of lemon juice and was formulated to balance Dr. Bronner's soaps.

Lemon juice works best for me. It's the middle weight. However, it has some drawbacks in that not everyone has an overflowing lemon tree in their yard. Plus, it takes time to juice and strain it so your husband isn't picking lemon pulp out of your hair for the rest of the day (speaking from experience here). Lemon juice also isn't shelf stable. It has to be kept in the fridge or it ferments. It's an extra step to have to swing by the kitchen to grab it before the shower.

Apple cider vinegar is the lightest of the three options and is best for fine hair. It is readily available, inexpensive, and shelf stable, so you can keep a bottle in your shower. Be sure to look for actual apple cider vinegar in stores, not "flavored" apple cider vinegar, which is distilled white vinegar with flavor and color added. I often use apple cider vinegar when lemon juice isn't handy.

Dr. Bronner's Citrus Organic Hair Rinse is the most intensely moisturizing option, best for drier or coarser hair. It contains not only the lemon juice to provide the smoothing acidity but also shikakai powder to nourish.

The transition to hair washing with soap takes time. The first time you wash your hair with soap, you're going to think it damaged your hair. However, that is not the case. If you've been using conventional shampoo and conditioner, you have a coating on your hair concealing its true state. The coating is usually made of quaternary ammonium compounds (quats) and silicone derivatives, such as dimethicone or siloxanes. Not only do these coatings cover up damage, but they can also impede scalp function. Soap reveals the true state of your hair by stripping away the coatings. If you get mad at the soap for the state of your hair, you're blaming the messenger.

When I first made the switch to soap, it took about two weeks for my hair to strengthen. I needed to do some hair masques (next section) and give my scalp time to wake up and do its job. The scalp should be the most lipid- (read "oil") producing skin on our bodies, but mine clearly was lying down on the job. After a couple weeks, though, it did get back in gear.

I've now been washing my hair with soap for well over a decade, and my hair is strong and healthy. I've also discovered something fun: my hair is wavy. When I used conventional products, my hair was so weighed down that it was more or less straight. Now I naturally have the so-called "beachy waves," which I like.

Gray and White Hair

Gray and white hair can be on the dry side because it no longer contains the melanin-rich pigment that contributes softness and pliability. To boost the moisture and soften hair, use the Organic Sugar Soap or Organic Shaving Soap. Gray and white hair tends to yellow. While I haven't had the opportunity to experience this effect for myself, I have heard from many customers who share that washing with the soaps has kept their whites and grays bright.

Colored Hair Caveats

If you've been on board with me so far, I might derail you with this last point: washing with soap is not advisable for conventionally colored hair. Dyes use alkalinity to open up the cuticles so that the dye saturates the inner cortex beneath the cuticle. The alkali most commonly used is ammonia, with a pH of 10. Soap, with its natural alkalinity, also opens these cuticles a bit and the dye may leach out.

There are two exceptions in which soap is still safe for colored hair. Pure henna dyes stain the keratin of the cuticles instead of being stored in the inner cortex. Soap is not detrimental to this dye. Also, if your hair is bleached or highlighted, where color is removed but not added, soap is still a great option.

WASHING HAIR WITH SOAP

HOW TO:

1. Using the Pure-Castile Liquid or Bar, Organic Sugar Soap, or Shaving Soap, work in enough soap to produce a nice lather. Massage through hair and scalp.

2. Rinse thoroughly.

3. Prepare a rinse of either 1 to 2 capfuls Dr. Bronner's Citrus Organic Hair Rinse in 1 cup (240 ml) water, apple cider vinegar diluted in half with water, or lemon juice diluted at 1 part lemon juice to 2 parts water. Pour this over your hair and work it through with your fingers.

4. Rinse out.

5. As a final step, after I towel dry my hair, I use a leave-in conditioner—a pump and a half of Dr. Bronner's Organic Hair Crème—worked mostly through the lower half of my hair where it is driest and most in need of moisturizing. The Organic Hair Crème is a lotion for hair. I then let my hair air dry to make my waves more pronounced. When I use a hairdryer or follow up with any sort of iron, the Organic Hair Crème acts as a heat protectant.

HAIR MASQUE

An occasional hair masque treatment brings deep moisture to hair. It is super helpful during the transition from shampoo to soap, to restore flexibility and shine. I also do a hair masque anytime I have my hair highlighted, which tends to strip out all the moisture. This is an alternative use I found for Dr. Bronner's Organic Hair Crème. Coconut oil also works.

Masques are most effective when done between washing and conditioning hair. You want to catch the hair when the soap has lifted the keratin scales at the surface of the hair strands so the masque can penetrate deeply into the inner cortex.

The hardest part is that the masque has to sit on the hair for 10 minutes, right in the middle of the shower. I pass the time by shaving or washing the shower, since I use the same Pure-Castile Soap on that, too. If this mid-shower masque really doesn't work for you, there is still benefit to doing a preshower masque.

HOW TO:

1. Wash hair with Pure-Castile or Organic Sugar Soap.

2. Rinse.

3. Apply Dr. Bronner's Organic Hair Crème or Virgin Coconut Oil to hair, concentrating most on the lower half and ends of hair. The amount is hugely dependent on hair type and length. For my long, medium to fine hair, I use about 1 tablespoon of the Organic Hair Crème or about a ½ teaspoon of the Virgin Coconut Oil. Use your fingers to work this through your hair, making sure it is all coated.

4. Let the masque sit on the hair for about 10 minutes. Twist long hair into a clip to keep the masque from dripping out.

5. After 10 minutes, rinse thoroughly with warm water.

6. Use one of the conditioning rinses as mentioned above: lemon juice, apple cider vinegar, or Dr. Bronner's Citrus Organic Hair Rinse.

After a hair masque, I do not use any more Organic Hair Crème on my hair that day. It doesn't need it. However, you do what works best for you.

Shaving

I have shaved with every Dr. Bronner's soap as well as our Virgin Coconut Oil. I use whatever is handiest. Michael sticks with the Pure-Castile Bar Soap. Whatever product you use, the technique is the same: Lather up the soap to a creamy texture and then apply the razor.

When my skin is particularly dry and ashy, I will shave with the Coconut Oil Sugar Scrub on page 58. This provides exfoliation plus moisture. I massage the scrub into my wet skin until the sugar dissolves, and then I apply the razor. The drawback to using coconut oil in the shower is that it can make the shower floor a little slippery. I combat this by making sure I don't use too much, and then if it is slick, I put a few drops of Pure-Castile Liquid Soap on my washcloth and swish that around the floor with my foot. Fancy, I know.

If needed after shaving, I apply either lotion, Virgin Coconut Oil, or Unscented Magic Balm, listed in increasing order of moisturizing intensity.

BEARD AND 'STACHE CARE

I have to speak from others' recommendations on this one, but I have been married to a beard for multiple decades. Pay attention to the ingredients in your beard and mustache products because they are right under your nose. Any fumes emitted are going to be inhaled immediately. Ingredients may even be ingested.

HOW TO:

1. Start by washing with the Pure-Castile Soap, either liquid or bar. If your facial hair is on the dryer side, use the Organic Sugar Soap instead and wash less frequently.

2. Tame, moisturize, and style with the Unscented Magic Balm, Organic Hair Crème, or Virgin Coconut Oil. The oils provide excellent nourishment to both skin and hair, and the beeswax of the Magic Balm gives a gentle hold.

Moisturizing

When I was in the midst of a frustrating teenage breakout, my mom first told me that breakouts can be a sign of dry skin. This stopped me in my tracks. Advertising had taught me that breakouts are caused by oily skin, so surely we need to be stripping our skin of oils and avoiding any oil-containing products. But Mom explained that dryness can cause skin to go into overdrive, cranking out oils in excess. How do moms know these things? She was absolutely correct. My relationship with moisturizers changed that day.

Moisturizing ingredients can be divided into three categories: occlusives, humectants, and emollients.

OCCLUSIVE: A barrier over the skin. It locks in moisture and wards off external hazards, such as wind and dust. Most oils, butters, and waxes act as occlusives.

HUMECTANT: Draws moisture into the skin and works best beneath the protection of an occlusive. Common simple humectants include gylcerin and sugars like honey and sucrose.[13]

EMOLLIENT: Replenishes lost lipids in the skin, filling in cracks and repairing damage.[14] There are two fatty acids that do this particularly well: linoleic and alpha-linolenic fatty acids, neither of which the body can produce on its own. This is why they are called essential fatty acids: we must eat them or apply them topically. They are readily found in safflower, grapeseed, sunflower, flaxseed, and hempseed oils.[15]

All three of these together produce the deepest moisturizing treatments. However, this might be too heavy if your skin is only mildly dry or if you're wearing it under makeup. In those cases, choose a moisturizer with perhaps just an emollient or just an occlusive.

The timing of moisturizing also matters. After bathing, pat the skin dry, but while it is still damp, apply your moisturizer. This helps lock in moisture that could be lost from evaporation. Also, use your sleeping time for heavier moisturizing treatments, especially on hands and feet.

Oils got a bad rap for comedogenicity a while back. That refers to how likely a product is to clog pores. A study done in the 1980s on rabbit ears produced a ranking of various oils that marketers jumped all over.[16] However, even at the time, scientists questioned the correlation between the reaction of rabbit skin and human skin.[17] Rabbit skin is far more sensitive. A follow-up study in 2006, this time on humans, found that the ingredients flagged as comedogenic were not necessarily so when tested on humans.[18] Find what works best for you.

As a final note on skin care, if your skin or hair ever undergoes a sudden, drastic change in appearance, or if your hair starts to fall out, this could be a sign of a serious medical condition. Please consult a medical professional.

GIY Scrubs

Skin-scrubbing products help exfoliate dead skin cells, which cause skin to appear ashy and be prone to cracks by reducing skin's suppleness. The first scrub I ever used was a gift from a friend, and I seriously could have eaten it: coconut oil, brown sugar, various cozy spices. It was some flour and an egg away from cookie dough.

Scrubs make excellent gifts and can be made of many different ingredients. You can customize the base by using grated Pure-Castile Bar Soap, liquid soap, or oil. You can customize the exfoliant by using sugar, salt, coffee grounds, or baking soda. You can personalize them further with essential oils, herbs, and spices. In all of my scrub combos below, you can make these swaps.

As you consider which exfoliant to use, bear in mind that the coarser the grain, the rougher the scrub. So, a sugar scrub made with the larger granules of raw sugar is going to give a more intense scrub than one made with superfine sugar, and so it should be reserved for rougher skin on feet and elbows. Also, if you opt to make your scrub from salt and soap, only use sodium chloride (sea salt or table salt). Don't mix Epsom salts with soap (see chart on page 77).

Here are five of my favorite GIY Scrub combos. Store scrubs in an airtight container.

SIMPLE SUGAR SOAP SCRUB

¼ cup (60 ml) Pure-Castile Liquid Soap in any scent or blend two 1¼ cups (250 g) granulated sugar

Mix the ingredients together with a fork until smooth.

COFFEE AND BAR SOAP SCRUB

This is a dry scrub that has a few advantages: it doesn't spill in travel or transport, it is concentrated and thus saves money, and it uses no plastic packaging. After brewing coffee, spread spent grounds on a plate to dry. You can vary the grind from a fine espresso to a coarse cold brew. This scrub has an extra superpower: coffee grounds remove odors, such as onions or garlic or acetone, from skin. I used my kitchen box grater to grate the Bar Soap, but a rotary cheese grater would be ideal.

⅔ cup (50 g) used, dry coffee grounds
⅔ cup (about 48 g) finely grated Almond Pure-Castile Bar Soap

Toss the two ingredients together. Use a small spoonful of the scrub at a time to prevent having too many coffee grounds go down the drain at once.

COCONUT OIL SUGAR SCRUB

⅔ cup (135 g) granulated sugar

¼ cup (60 ml) Virgin Coconut Oil (liquid)

20 to 30 drops essential oils (optional)

Combine the ingredients in a bowl with a fork to break up lumps.

PEPPERMINT AND COCONUT OIL FOOT SCRUB

This combination of sugar and oil uses the coarser turbinado sugar and is best for feet or other very thick skin. The peppermint makes it incredibly refreshing. Apply it to feet with a pumice stone.

⅔ cup (150 g) turbinado sugar (aka "raw sugar")

¼ cup (60 ml) coconut oil gently melted to a liquid

20 drops peppermint essential oil

Combine the ingredients in a bowl with a fork to break up lumps.

ORIGIN STORY:
Organic Magic Balms

A small aluminum tub appeared on my bathroom counter one day, with "v. 12" scribbled in marker on the lid. Trusting soul that I am, I assumed it was something someone sent me from Dr. Bronner's HQ that I was supposed to check out. So, I opened the lid, took a big sniff, and nearly landed on the floor.

This was my introduction to the Arnica-Menthol Organic Magic Balm.

I guessed that this was an alternative to the petroleum-based Vicks VapoRub. It had the same powerhouse of mentholated vapors. Another colleague supposed it was a sore foot rub. Turned out my brother David concocted this for his own after-surfing use on sore muscles. It is all that and more.

Though the two scents of the Organic Magic Balm—the Unscented and the Arnica-Menthol—have the exact same base, their uses are rarely interchangeable. Where the Unscented is soothing and mellow, the Arnica-Menthol is energizing and refreshing.

What I love most about the Magic Balms is their simplicity. (Who's surprised?) The Magic Balm base—which is all that's in the Unscented Balm—has seven ingredients. I can remember seven. Five oils, one wax, one antioxidant. And each ingredient is edible. (Don't eat the balm. I'm making the point that it's healthy.) When I travel, I always take these two with me for any little surprises. What one balm doesn't alleviate, the other one likely does.

More Uses for Dr. Bronner's Organic Magic Balm and Lip Balm

UNSCENTED ORGANIC MAGIC BALM

+ Soften rough skin on elbows and feet. This is especially effective right after a shower or bath.
+ Prevent chafing prior to running, boogie boarding, or other activities.
+ Soothe skin grazes by gently coating roughened skin.
+ Coat irritated, red noses and cheeks for protection and prevention.
+ For a dewy glow on cheeks or eyelids, dab a bit blended with a touch of powdered makeup for color.
+ Condition eyelashes with an overnight masque.
+ Prevent hair dye from staining skin by applying a layer along your hairline prior to the dye treatment.

ARNICA-MENTHOL ORGANIC MAGIC BALM

+ Use as a massage oil (or customize your own scent by blending a few drops of your favorite essential oil into the Unscented Balm).
+ Cool the irritation of bug bites.
+ Apply to your chest and neck when you're congested.
+ Energize tired feet.

ORGANIC LIP BALM

+ Solve the dilemma of lip balm or lip color by using the Organic Lip Balm as a lip tint. For deep color, line lips thickly with lip liner, then blend the color with the lip balm. For a subtler color, apply the lip balm first and then line lips with the liner.
+ Tame, style, and nourish eyebrows with the lip balms. Swipe balm over the brows and style with a spoolie brush.
+ Work into hard, cracked cuticles, ideally right before bedtime. The thick formula stays put to protect and soften.
+ Prior to applying nail polish, coat the cuticles with lip balm so that any polish overflow does not adhere to skin.
+ Tame hair flyaways with a quick swipe of the lip balm.

Foot Rejuvenation

There is nothing so relieving to the feet as soaking them in a basin of water with a good squirt of the Peppermint Pure-Castile Soap. Use hot (not scalding) water for end-of-the-day relaxation or cold water on hot days for deep cooling. Wiggle your toes and flex your ankles to work out all the kinks. Then give them a scrub with the Peppermint Foot Scrub (above) and rinse. Follow this up with an ample application of Arnica-Menthol Balm, massaging it into the tendons and muscles as well as the toughened skin of the heels and toes. Don a pair of comfy socks for the night, and your feet—and you—will wake up feeling like they've been on vacation.

LAB COAT MOMENT
"Freezing" Soap

Although many homemade foot and body soaks call for mixing Castile soap and Epsom salts, you'll see why this is not a good idea. Fill a clear glass with ½ cup (120 ml) of water. Add 1 teaspoon of Epsom salts and stir until fully dissolved. Pour 1 teaspoon (5 ml) of Pure-Castile Liquid Soap into the water. Do not stir it. Observe the soap instantly "freeze" midswirl, like someone hit the pause button in an action sequence. Why is this? Consider that Epsom salts are magnesium sulfate. Magnesium reacts readily with a true soap such as the Pure-Castile, forming a semisolid, harmless substance chemically called "magnesium cocoate" but that we commonly call soap scum. Yes, I just had you make soap scum on purpose. I want you to see that chemistry happens, and it's neat to see the soap transform so fast. You don't want this coating your tub and your pipes. For this reason, *do not pour this mixture down your drain.* Instead, line a sieve with a paper towel. Hold the sieve over a sink and slowly pour the solution through in order to collect the solids. Then throw the paper towel in the trash or compost.

Hand and Nail Treatment

At the end of the day, massage the Coconut Oil Sugar Scrub thoroughly into your hands, concentrating on hardened or cracking areas. Rinse your hands in warm water and pat dry.

Then, massage in some Unscented Magic Balm and cover your hands with cotton gloves overnight. Your hands will look as good as new in the morning.

For cuticles, soften them overnight by applying Naked Unscented Organic Lip Balm generously just before crawling into bed. Then, in the morning before you head into your day, massage a bit of coconut oil into the nails for a healthy, nourishing shine.

Tattoo Care

New tattoos need to be kept clean and protected while they heal. Because the skin is sensitive, the Unscented Pure-Castile Soap is best due to its lack of essential oils and double ratio of olive oil. Plus, this soap leaves no residues to irritate the raw skin.

Protect the healing skin with the Unscented Magic Balm. The beeswax, coconut, jojoba, and avocado oils are all occlusives, forming that protective barrier over the skin. Further, the Unscented Magic Balm is free of alcohol and fragrance, both of which can dry and irritate healing skin, and free of petroleum, which the American Academy of Dermatology says can cause ink fade.[19]

For existing tattoos, use one of the sugar scrubs to exfoliate any dead skin. Then, massage either the Unscented Magic Balm or Virgin Coconut Oil to keep your skin nourished and the colors vibrant.

Oral Care

Oral care is a unique category because our mouths are at the transition point between internal and external. We must assume that anything we use in our mouths has the potential to be ingested. Also, the skin in our mouth is thinner, which makes it more sensitive. Healthy ingredients are paramount. Furthermore, oral appliances tend to be custom and pricey. We want to care for them in ways that help them last a good many years.

Brushing Teeth

Teeth brushing was one of my grandfather's original uses for the Pure-Castile Soap. Indeed it does work just fine, except that it tastes like soap. Nonetheless, if you are looking for an abrasive-free option for teeth cleaning, or if you are in a situation where you need to pare down products to the barest minimum—such as when backpacking—the Pure-Castile is there for you. Use one drop on your toothbrush. But when in 2015 we released the All-One Toothpaste, my voice was among the joyous throngs.

Culturally we are accustomed to very foamy toothpastes, which is only possible with synthetic detergents and foaming agents that are not best for our mouths. Foam, or rather the bubbles that constitute foam, do not indicate cleaning power. Cleaning happens through micelle formation, which I'll get to later. Foaming is purely a psychological connection we have with cleaning. Now that I am used to a low-foaming toothpaste, I find conventional toothpastes almost suffocating in their foam volume. With 70 percent organic content and the absence of synthetic detergents, dyes, or flavors, the All-One Toothpaste will clean your mouth with just a pea-sized amount of paste. The toothpaste packs a punch of flavor with essential oils and menthol crystals. If breaking up with foam is a tough hurdle, add one drop of Castile to your brush as well.

CLEANING DENTURES

We used to joke with my grandfather that he advocated brushing teeth with the Pure-Castile Soap because he was able to take his teeth out of his mouth before doing so.

Pure-Castile Soap is an effective denture cleaner and does not have the downsides of other options. Sodium hypochlorite—aka chlorine bleach—can roughen surfaces and deteriorate resin materials in dentures.[20] Both bleach and denture-cleansing tablets have been shown to corrode metals used in partial dentures.[21] *Abrasives such as toothpastes or baking soda can cause wear.*

Since the American Dental Association lists both mild hand soap and dishwashing liquid among its recommendations for denture cleaning, Pure-Castile Soap and Dr. Bronner's Sal Suds Biodegradable Cleaner (tons more on this later) are interchangeable options.

HOW TO:

1. After removing the dentures from your mouth, rinse them under running water to remove debris.

2. Apply 2–3 drops of Pure-Castile Soap, 1 drop of Sal Suds, or swipe a soft toothbrush over a bar of soap reserved for this purpose.

3. Brush dentures thoroughly.

4. Rinse well.

Dentures should be stored in fresh water when not in use to maintain their shape and keep from drying out.

CLEANING ORAL APPLIANCES

Retainers, sports guards, headgear, teeth-whitening trays, or the night-guard I've worn to sleep for years can all be kept clean by brushing them daily with the Pure-Castile Soap or Sal Suds. For all the reasons I mention above regarding dentures, avoid using bleach, toothpaste, or baking soda for these devices.

HOW TO:

1. Wet the device.

2. Apply 1 or 2 drops of Pure-Castile Soap—or I use one squirt from my foaming pump—or 1 drop of Sal Suds to a soft toothbrush.

3. Brush gently but thoroughly and rinse well.

4. Let the device air dry unless the manufacturer says to keep it submerged.

Caring for Babies, Children, and Individuals with Sensitive Skin

It was my brother Mike who first opened my eyes to the lack of oversight for cosmetics in general and baby products in particular. He was giving a presentation to my Mothers of Preschoolers (MOPS) group at my invitation. Others probably thought his info was old news to me, but it wasn't. I was just as rapt and appalled as they were. Everything I've already mentioned— the lack of safety testing, the prevalence of endocrine disruptors and allergens and sensitizers, and worse, the reactive rather than proactive nature of the whole system—made me feel like my children and I were guinea pigs in a giant science experiment. On the rare occasions that there is a regulation regarding body care products, it is only *after* an ingredient has been in circulation for a while and had some negative impact on the public. Because of this, there are many ingredients that, despite study after study emphasizing their hazards, are still ubiquitous in personal care products. Further, in the United States, cosmetics and personal care products are consistently the leading cause of poison exposure in children under six.[22]

As my brother spoke, I absorbed the sobering thought that no one has my loved ones' best interests at heart as much as I do. It was a disillusioning realization, and for a while I felt a crushing weight: "It's all up to me." This fueled my deep dive into personal care products and cosmetic chemistry, initially for my own benefit and eventually in my writing for others.

Mike's presentation opened my eyes to how important it is to analyze the products we're using on our children. There's nothing about products marketed for babies and children that makes them any safer than those marketed for adults. Below I talk about body and skin care for babies—and for pregnant and new mothers. These tips are valid for anyone with sensitivities or who wants to dial things back to the absolute simplest in their products.

Unscented Organic Magic Balm for Pregnancy, Postpartum, and Babies

With its short but rich list of ingredients, this balm has all it needs for delicate or depleted skin and nothing more. No fragrance, no alcohols, no synthetics. Nourishing and mild. I wish this formulation had been developed in time for me to use on my littles, but it has still been much used through their older years. We each have our own tub, labeled of course. I regularly add it to baby shower gifts for friends now.

For Pregnancy

Had this balm existed when I was pregnant, I would have saturated myself with it.

+ Relieve itchy bellies: apply directly after a shower to lock in moisture.
+ Relax sore feet: rub a few drops of your favorite pregnancy-approved essential oil into the balm to ease aching feet. A few drops of peppermint make a nice option.
+ Enjoy all-over massage: I had a pregnancy massage late in my firstborn's gestation. It was a beautiful thing.

For Postpartum

+ Relieve sore skin: so much of the body needs to heal, and this balm can keep skin supple as it does so.
+ Soothe nipples as they acclimate to nursing: apply to sore, cracked nipples. Discuss wiping off before nursing with your medical provider.

For Babies and Children

+ Create a barrier between skin and wet or soiled diapers: apply a thin layer after each diaper change. Pure Virgin Coconut Oil also works well for this.
+ Prevent angry red creases: apply behind the knees, under the neck, and in all the adorable chubby little folds to keep them from chafing and turning red.

✦ Relieve chapped skin: apply to cheeks and hands chapped by extreme weather and moisture loss.
✦ Soften behind the ears: apply to crusty areas behind the ears to soften and remove dead skin buildup.
✦ Prevent chafing: apply prior to potentially chafing activities: running, boogie boarding, skiing, life in general.

Washing Babies

I'm going to start out this baby-washing section with an odd exhortation: don't wash them too often. Babies don't need whole-body daily washings. Every time we wash them, it strips their skin of oils. And babies don't get that dirty, especially with the regular diaper cleanings, which already clean the most soiled parts. Even when you do wash them, they don't need that much of a cleanser. On the delicate skin of the face, pure water is best, with no cleanser at all.

If it's the relaxation of bath time before bedtime that your little one craves, there are ways to create that soothing rhythm:

✦ Enjoy water play with no soap, just a couple inches of water and your constant presence.
✦ Do a massage with a warm cloth or a bit of the Unscented Organic Magic Balm.
✦ Develop a wind-down routine that doesn't involve bathing: brush teeth, wipe the face and hands, read, sing, rock, snuggle.

Lest you come to the conclusion from the above that I didn't bathe my babies, let me assure you that I did. I washed my babies with the Pure-Castile Soap. Sometimes liquid. Sometimes bar. Sometimes Baby Unscented, sometimes Almond or Lavender. I held off on the Peppermint because I figured the menthol activation would startle them.

What I didn't use was any "tear-free" formulation, for reasons I discuss below. Even though I'm not a "tear-free" proponent, I will douse a persistent myth about tear-free products: they do not, and never have, contained numbing agents. I don't know where this idea started, but I've heard it a lot. Stop and think about it, though. If tear-free products contained an eye-numbing concentration of lidocaine or some other numbing agent, it would numb more than the baby's eyes. It would numb their entire bodies and the hands that washed the baby. I think baby washers everywhere would have noticed.

PURE-CASTILE SOAP FOR BABIES

I used the Pure-Castile Soap because it is super mild with its "best-for-skin" blend of saponified oils. Because it has a mildly alkaline pH, it is not "tear-free," so I used a washcloth as a way to control the soap on the baby and as a way not to use too much soap. You will notice that Pure-Castile Soap does not bubble as much as synthetic detergents. This does not mean a lack of cleaning power. Bubbles have nothing to do with cleaning power, but their abundance does mark the presence of artificial foaming agents that are not best for babies' skin.

I can only imagine how many different methodologies there are for washing babies. I do not pretend that this is the only best method, but here's how I washed mine.

HOW TO:

1. Wipe the baby's face with a cloth dampened only with water.

2. Moisten the baby's hair with a water-wet washcloth.

3. On the washcloth, apply one of the following:
   a. a few drops of Pure-Castile Liquid Soap
   b. one pump of a foaming dilution of Pure-Castile Liquid Soap
   c. one swipe of Pure-Castile Bar Soap

4. Wash the baby's hair with the washcloth. Rinse out the washcloth and then rinse the baby's hair with the wet washcloth.

5. Reapply a small amount of soap to the washcloth. Wash the rest of the baby, rinsing with a water-wet washcloth.

NOTE: An acidic rinse is not needed on baby hair. The texture of their hair does not require it. I didn't need to use it on my kids until around age 5 or 6, when their hair became a little coarser.

GIY BABY WIPES (NOT JUST FOR BABIES)

These wipes are also just the thing for wiping sticky hands or faces, and they certainly aren't only for babies. Even when I would drop the kids off at middle school, I'd often hand out these wipes for sticky faces.

> 1½ cup (360 ml) warm water
>
> 1 teaspoon (5 ml) Baby Unscented Pure-Castile Liquid Soap
>
> 1½ tablespoons (22.5 ml) Virgin Coconut Oil, warmed to a liquid
>
> Essential oils of your choice, no more than 15 drops (optional)

HOW TO:

1. Add all of the ingredients to a jar.

2. Close it and shake well to combine.

The purpose of the oil in this solution is to provide lubrication for the wipe so that it glides smoothly over the baby's skin. As I'll get into later, combining soap with oil only binds the soap to the oil. In this case, I am using that combination for lubrication.

FOR DISPOSABLE WIPES: Cut a paper towel roll in half using an electric kitchen knife. Place the half roll in a jar—I found a glass cookie jar or a pickle jar worked perfectly—and pour the solution over it. After a few minutes, the central cardboard tube will soften and you can pull it out. Dispense wipes from the middle.

FOR REUSABLE WIPES: Pour solution into a small spray bottle. You may need to swirl the solution a bit at each use. Spray baby's bottom and wipe with a soft cloth, or place soft cloths in a container or wipe warmer and pour solution over them.

8 Tips for Choosing Better Baby Products

I look over this list and there's not one point here that doesn't also hold true for buying products for any other life stage. While the stakes are heightened with babies and their rapidly developing and vulnerable little systems, these are valid principles for anyone. Studies continue to startle us as they reveal what baby and children's products contain: potentially hazardous volatile organic compounds, endocrine disruptors, phthalates, parabens, and 1,4-dioxane.[23] Our best response: simplify, simplify, simplify. Babies don't need much. Pour on the love. Not the products.

1. Buy less. *Choose . . . fewer products, with short, simple ingredient lists.*
   Before you load up on baby wash, shampoo, bubble bath, lotion, oil, powder, and cream, think of the sheer number of ingredients contained in that lot. That's a lot to monitor. Using fewer products on your baby means less to track. This can be tough amid the barrage of baby marketing and "essential" baby products. Just say no. Your baby doesn't need a full beauty regimen. Where there is a need, address it, but otherwise, skip all the products and pour on the cuddles.

2. Skip artificial fragrance. *Choose . . . unscented or scented lightly with essential oils.*
   Whether it's baby wipes, soap, laundry detergent, or diaper cream, fragrance is immaterial to effectiveness. As I explained earlier, the word "fragrance" can hide a range of ingredients, and the developing systems of babies are particularly sensitive to them. Among the possibilities are sensitizers, allergens, and phthalates, which studies are starting to link to everything from male infertility to neurological disorders.

3. Skip powder. *Choose . . . a simple balm to prevent chafing.*
   I know I'm battling nostalgia here, but any powder poses a known inhalation risk, whether it is talcum powder or cornstarch.[24] Through overzealous application or accidental exposure (a baby playing with a bottle of powder), both substances have caused instances of severe respiratory

distress requiring intubation, steroids, admission to the pediatric ICU, and antibiotics. While cornstarch has been proffered as a safer alternative to talcum powder, both pose the same inhalation risk.

4. Skip dyes. *Choose . . . dye-free formulations.*

Dyes are not functional components of any baby products, so you're not giving up any utility by avoiding them. Many dyes used in baby products are derived from petrochemicals with endearing names such as FD&C Blue No. 4 or D&C Yellow No. 10. While they receive FDA certification, many—including the two I just mentioned—are not approved for use around the eyes. Also, even while giving certification, the FDA cautions that certain dyes, such as "FD&C Yellow No. 5 may cause itching and hives in some people."[25] Despite these known risks, these dyes are still found in numerous baby shampoos and bubble baths.

5. Skip parabens, quaternium compounds, urea compounds. *Choose . . . products with tocopherols (vitamin E).*

The ingredients to skip are preservatives, in part. Certain parabens are being increasingly linked to hormone disruption and are showing up in breast cancer tumors. As aforementioned, both quaternium compounds and urea release formaldehyde, and while formaldehyde is a known human carcinogen, the more substantiated and immediately noticeable problem is that 1 in 12 people in the United States has a contact allergy to formaldehyde or with repeated exposure will develop one.[26] Of formaldehyde releasers in cosmetics, quaternium-15 has been found to release the most formaldehyde. In lieu of these, tocopherols are antioxidants that capture free oxygen molecules that hasten oxidation. Safflower and sunflower oils are concentrated sources. The tocopherols Dr. Bronner's uses are derived from the latter.

6. Skip the assurance of "tear-free." *Choose . . . a cleanser with a healthy ingredient list and use only water to clean your baby's face.*

"Tear-free" is a commentary on the product's eye-irritation potential

continues

and does not speak to whether the ingredients are healthy. Many "tear-free" products contain synthetic detergents, which are not the best for baby's skin and carry other risks, even though they may not irritate the eyes. Common are ethoxylated compounds, such as sodium laureth sulfate or polyethylene glycol (PEG), which can be contaminated with the potentially cancer causing 1,4-dioxane.[27] Propylene glycol is another red flag, a penetration enhancer, and flagged by the CDC as an irritant.[28] Cocamidopropyl betaine makes the top 10 causes of allergic contact dermatitis by the American Academy of Dermatology.[29] All of these are commonly found in tear-free baby products.

7. Skip the sunscreen on newborns and the oxybenzone and octinoxate at any age. *Choose. . . shade and light coverings until 6 months. Afterward, use mineral-based lotion sunscreens alongside other sun prevention, such as shade and skin-covering ultraviolet protection factor (UPF) fabrics.* Both the sun and sunscreen are too potent for newborns to face, and many common sunscreen active ingredients—such as oxybenzone and octinoxate—aren't safe for anyone. All six of the most common chemical sunscreen active ingredients (avobenzone, oxybenzone, octocrylene, homosalate, octisalate, and octinoxate) have been shown to absorb into the body's bloodstream and remain in the body for extended periods of time.[30] There are only two sunscreen ingredients that the FDA has proposed giving GRASE (Generally Regarded as Safe and Effective) status to: the minerals zinc oxide and titanium dioxide.[31] Propylene glycol, mentioned above, is also common in baby- and kid-marketed sunscreens.

8. Skip "baby" laundry detergents and any fabric softeners. *Choose . . . a clean-rinsing, dye-free, scent-free soap or mild detergent. Add baking soda for extra scrubbing and deodorizing, and/or pure white vinegar to the rinse cycle for fabric softening.* There is nothing about the word "baby" on a product that makes it any safer for babies. There is no regulation or requirement for using that word. What is best for babies is also what is best for adult clothes: tough on stains, exceedingly clean rinsing, dye-free, and fragrance-free.

Ask Lisa

Q What soap should I use for my acne/rosacea/psoriasis/redness/imbalanced skin?

A While the Pure-Castile Soap cannot replace the advice of your doctor, it can pair up alongside it. The benefit of Pure-Castile Soap to troubled skin is that it is simple. I know I'm being repetitive, but that's what we keep coming back to. There are no synthetic ingredients, no unnecessary ingredients that may cast a wider net of allergens—no colorants, no foaming agents, no thickeners, no fillers. It leaves no residues. The Baby Unscented Pure-Castile Soap is the mildest of all, with the Tea Tree Pure-Castile Soap right next to it.

Q Why is the word "fragrance" in your Almond and Rose Pure-Castile Soaps when you've said to be wary of the word?

A Excellent! Yes, this is exactly the sort of question you should ask when you see the word "fragrance." For the Almond Pure-Castile, the beloved scent that we call "almond"—that warm marzipan and amaretto coziness—comes from a naturally occurring compound called benzaldehyde. Benzaldehyde occurs naturally in all stone fruits, including almonds, peaches, apricots, plums, cherries, and also in the oil of the *Cinnamomum cassia* tree.

Dr. Bronner's uses benzaldehyde from cassia bark oil, instead of from almond or other stone fruit, for two reasons. First, benzaldehyde from bitter almond oil, which is what comes from any stone fruit, also contains prussic acid, better known as the poison cyanide. This must be refined out of the oil, an extra step that reduces output. Secondly, the cassia tree grows readily in tropical climates with little human input, whereas stone fruits require far more intensive cultivation and water.

All in all, cassia-derived benzaldehyde is a more efficient and sustainable option. Why the scent of benzaldehyde got named "almond" in our cultural

continues

heads when it occurs in such a variety of plants, I cannot begin to guess. Someone somewhere had the privilege of naming, and the name stuck.

The Rose Pure-Castile also lists the word "fragrance" in its ingredients. This is for a different reason. The scent of the Rose Pure-Castile is a blend of various floral essential oils, not just rose. This is partially for cost—pure rose oil at over $900/ounce, would price the soap out of range for even the most devoted users—but also because the blend of florals, which includes geranium, rosemary, grapefruit, and orange, produces a much more complex profile.

Q **Are the Tea Tree Pure-Castile and Lavender Pure-Castile soaps safe for children?**

A This question has popped up in waves over the years, and it all stems from a paper written back in 2007 about four boys with prepubertal gynecomastia, which is the appearance of breast tissue before the onset of puberty. The author concluded that this was due to exposure to tea tree and lavender essential oils, a conclusion that was immediately and repeatedly denounced because of the few cases and non-consideration of other causes. In 2022 a sizable study of 556 children exposed to these two oils concluded that they were no more likely to develop any evidence of endocrine (hormone) disruptions than children who were not.[32]

Q **Are the essential oils in Dr. Bronner's soaps safe during pregnancy?**

A Yes, the soap formulations with their essential oils are safe during pregnancy. The cautions you may hear regarding the use of essential oils during pregnancy are addressing the concentrated use of essential oils in leave-on applications. In Dr. Bronner's Pure-Castile soaps, the maximum concentration of essential oils is 2 percent. Further consider that soap is a wash-off product, so there is not the same opportunity for exposure as with a leave-on application.

All that being said, anyone can be sensitive to anything. Just because it's not a common allergen doesn't mean it doesn't adversely impact a person.

Use what is best for your body and mind. The most conservative route would be to use the Baby Unscented.

Q **How do I add essential oils to the Pure-Castile Soaps?**

A This is a great way to customize a scent. You can start with the Baby Unscented to make a scent that is completely your own or modify one of the other scents with an addition of your choice. You can scent either a whole undiluted bottle of soap or one of the many dilutions. Start by adding just a few drops and swirl. Essential oils go a long way, and different essential oils have different strengths. Where you might use 20 drops of one, you might get your desired scent level with five drops of another. So start with fewer drops and increase based on your preference. Swirl thoroughly after each addition. If the soap sits for several days, you may find you need to swirl in the essential oils again. When purchasing essential oils, look for organic pure essential oil. If it doesn't say "pure essential," then it is diluted in some other carrier oil, like olive oil. Mixing two Pure-Castile Soap scents is another way to create a custom scent.

Q **Can I mix Pure-Castile Soap with . . .? (Bathroom Edition)**

A One category of questions I have received more than I expected is the "can I mix" questions. All these ingredient options are from reader questions. I have an additional list related to house care in The Cleaning Cabinet.

The short story is: chemistry happens. Ingredients can react with each other. In the chart below, I review the ingredients I've been asked about when combined with Dr. Bronner's Pure-Castile Soap.

Ingredient Combinations with Dr. Bronner's Pure-Castile Soap

INGREDIENT	INTENT	USE WITH PURE-CASTILE?	ELABORATION
Aloe vera	To soothe skin	No	Aloe vera brings greatest benefit to the skin when it is allowed to sit on the skin for a period of time. Soap, as a wash-off product, is in contact with the skin so briefly that the aloe vera won't have the opportunity to be beneficial. It is better to apply aloe after washing.
Citric acid	Lower the pH	No	Acid will react with the soap itself and break apart the soap molecule. You'll be left with an oily mess. The observant reader will say, "But your ingredients list citric acid!" Yes, we add carefully apportioned amounts of citric acid to balance the pH. Adding any more citric acid than we've already added will reverse the saponification reaction.
Coconut milk	To make a more moisturizing soap	No	Mixing coconut milk and Pure-Castile Soap will make a pleasingly creamy liquid that seems like it would be nourishing. However, it is an illusion. The high oil content in coconut milk means the soap will be latching on to these oils. The soap will then not be available to cleanse, and the coconut milk will not be available to moisturize. See the discussion of oils below.

INGREDIENT	INTENT	USE WITH PURE-CASTILE?	ELABORATION
Epsom salts	To incorporate potential relaxation and anti-inflammatory benefits of Epsom salts	No	Epsom salts are magnesium sulfate. Magnesium reacts readily with a true soap such as castile. This combo will leave heavy residues on tubs and in plumbing. Soak in Epsom salts before or after you bathe with soap but not at the same time.
Glycerin	To make the soap more moisturizing and to make bubbles	Yes	There is already naturally occurring glycerin in Dr. Bronner's Pure-Castile Soap, but if you would like to add more, go for it. There is no adverse reaction.
Colloidal oatmeal	To harness oatmeal's anti-inflammatory, antihistaminic, skin soothing, and moisturizing properties[33]	Yes	Colloidal oatmeal is made by grinding rolled oats into a very fine powder. There is no reaction between Pure-Castile Soap and oatmeal. Be sure the oatmeal is very diluted so as not to clog drains. If you're making a skin poultice, throw it away in the trash can when done rather than rinsing it down the drain.
Any oil (jojoba, olive, coconut, shea butter, etc.)	To make a more moisturizing cleanser	No	Soap's primary purpose is to latch on to oils and wash them away. If you directly add oil to soap, the soap will get to work surrounding the added oil molecules and will no longer be available to clean your skin. And with all the soap molecules hanging on to them, the oils will not be available to moisturize. Moisturize after cleansing.

INGREDIENT	INTENT	USE WITH PURE-CASTILE?	ELABORATION
Table salt or sea salt (sodium chloride)	To exfoliate	Yes	There is no reaction between sodium chloride and Pure-Castile Soap. Keep in mind that the larger the salt crystal, the rougher the scrub. Use finer crystals on more delicate skin and larger crystals on tougher skin, such as that of the elbows and feet.
Sugar (cane, honey, sucrose, etc.)	To exfoliate and draw moisture into the skin	Yes	You can make a lovely scrub by mixing sugar or honey with Pure-Castile Soap.
Vitamin E (mixed tocopherols)	To extend the shelf life of a solution	Yes, but . . .	Mixed tocopherols—aka vitamin E—are the antioxidants we use in our soaps to protect their shelf life. They capture any free oxygen from oils and prevent rancidity. They are neither antibacterial agents nor preservatives so adding them to a water dilution, such as for a foaming pump, provides no benefit.

CHAPTER 2

THE CLEANING CABINET

I feel like the maid; I just cleaned up this mess!
Can we keep it clean for 10 minutes?
— MR. INCREDIBLE

Mocha brown eyes gazed somberly up at me above softly rounded cheeks and rosy red lips, which were firmly wrapped around the square green plastic nozzle of a bottle of Formula 409.

Emotions poured through me as I snatched the bottle from my two-year-old son: surprise, fear, frustration, guilt, uncertainty, anger, inadequacy. I promptly called Poison Control.

We were now a statistic. One of the 124,934 calls made to Poison Control in 2008 for accidental exposure to household cleaning products in children under six.

Poison Control turned out to be no help because, at the time, the ingredients in cleaning solutions were not disclosed, instead concealed as proprietary knowledge. The advisor had no more idea what my son had ingested than I did. With the lackluster advice to "keep an eye on him, and if he has problems take him to the ER" echoing in my ears, I realized I was the one with a problem.

He had come up behind me when I had thought he was napping and of course went right for the worst possible, though most intriguing, object.

So much for stealth cleaning. The whole reason I was spending these precious naptime moments cleaning was to avoid the risk of chemical exposure to the kids. But why should I even have to do that? Cleaning, which is ostensibly for our health and well-being, shouldn't be something I have to do on the sly so that no one gets hurt.

What was I going to do now?

In that moment, one thing was abundantly clear. To ensure the safety and well-being of myself and my family, I had work to do. My green journey had begun.

Perhaps you've had a 409 Moment or two of your own. A hinge moment when, in a split second, life alters. An accident, a health revelation, a sudden conviction that spurred you to change.

My son, who now towers over me, is perfectly fine. There was no damage from that 409 Moment. In the realm of conventional products, 409 is by far not the worst, but what if in my well-meaning desire to have a clean house, I had been using a far more caustic cleaner at that moment, like an oven or toilet bowl cleaner?

After that near-miss, the top priority for me became products that cleaned effectively by the least intensive means, whose ingredients I understood, whose fumes and residues would not harm me or those around me, and even when misused by curious two-year-olds, would not cause injury.

Let's step back a moment and think about cleaning as a concept. I've come up with something I call The Law of Conservation of Dirt: dirt is neither created nor destroyed. It is merely moved from one place to another.

From the counter to the rag. From the floor to the mop. Sometimes I wonder how often I've moved the same dirt.

I was lamenting this very thing to Michael during our breakfast one day. We have found breakfast is our best time to connect with each other. When the weather's nice and the sun is up, we sit on the porch to soak in the rhythms of the waking world before diving into our mostly indoor professions.

I was frustrated one day because I had so many things to do that I had recently done. Pay bills, do laundry, mop floors, tend kids, meet work deadlines, deal with our puppy jumping over the fence. Why can't tasks get done and stay done?

Our day was awaiting, so with a raised eyebrow and a sideways smile, Michael got up and wished me luck with managing my blessings.

That right there. Such a typical Michael maneuver. He grabs my framed picture of the world and flips it upside down. Maybe it's because he's left-handed that he does this so well.

He walked me to other side of my situation to see the life full of vibrance and abundance and adventure. Because he's right, of course. These are blessings. Every one of them, and short-lived ones at that. Kids will soon all be grown and flown and no one will be around to mess up the house. Work opportunities may fade, and the puppy will become sedate and predictable. I'll miss that white and brown canine streak gleefully flying by the front window, giving me occasion to breathe some fresh air and get to know my neighbors.

Michael has always had that impact on me. He helps me see the world from a different angle, and I think he has appreciated that I've let him. It's part of how we fit together. The first thing I ever did to impress him was let him teach me to count in binary: 1, 10, 11, 100 . . . . Binary aside, it was not love at first sight between us. For one thing, he was old—25 to my mere 19. Plus, we were both on self-imposed breaks from relationships. And he had a beard.

We met in Mexico City in the summer of 1996 in a program working through churches with children and youth. The first inkling I had that perhaps there might be something more between us was when I received word from home, via my weekly call from the corner pay phone, that my grandfather was not doing well. My grandfather, Dr. Bronner. He's not easy to describe to someone for the first time, and it was harder for me back then, before I knew exactly where I fit in to the family story or even how I felt about it all.

"I have this grandfather who went blind because of the electroshock therapy he experienced in a mental institution, which he eventually escaped from and hitchhiked to California and started a soap company for the purpose of distributing a message about world peace because his parents died in the Holocaust and he's concerned about nuclear proliferation and water fluoridation, and the soap's really popular among hippies and backpackers. And he has Parkinson's."

Um, yeah.

But Michael suggested we have coffee to talk about it. That's the moment it all began. Our us-ness. If that didn't scare him off, he was something to hold on to. We married two years later.

Seven years into our marriage, we moved to California, a development that had not been on our long-term radar when we started together. Within a few years, he became chief operations officer overseeing a team that has swelled from 35 to hundreds in the production of a company that grew from $15 million in annual sales to several hundred million. His ability to take things in stride, from a crusading grandfather-in-law to a global pandemic, has served him well through it all.

One hiccup we faced at about this time is that I had experienced this revelatory green wake-up call, but Michael had not. I know I'm not alone in this. I've heard the question many a time, "How do I get my spouse/roommate/parents/children/boss with me on the green train?"

Michael and I had to walk that road, too. Just like any other topic when companions are in different places, we needed to remember that we have far more in common than not, and to keep lines of communication open. Looking back, here are some things I learned about transitioning to GIY cleaning products:

1. **Don't throw out the stuff they're comfortable with.** The Formula 409 stayed for a while, though I might have made it harder to access. But it was there on a high shelf in the garage, "just in case," a token of peace.

2. **Make it easy to switch.** I made the GIY products easy to grab and posted the Dilution Cheat Sheets in the cleaning cabinet.[34]

3. **Model it.** This meant I did more of the cleaning for a bit, but it demonstrated that the GIY products worked.

4. **Listen.** He had valid concerns. Will they work? Would our house be sanitary?

5. **Value his gradual change.** My own change had taken some time, as would his.

6. **Be gracious. Be patient.** Just as others have shown me grace, it's my turn to extend the same to him.

7. **Be positive.** No one likes a nag. Nagging is not convincing.

8. **Timing is everything.** Running out the door is not the right moment to talk about green cleaning. Nor is lying in bed at the end of an exhausting day. Nor when you're hungry.

9. **Admit I don't know it all and am still learning.** This was honest.

10. **Notice.** When he gave it a try, I let him know I appreciated his effort.

It's funny to think about all this now. In many ways Michael is now more of a stickler than I am. Pity the landscaper who tries to use glyphosate (Roundup) in our yard.

Happily, since my own heart-stopping beginning, not only has my knowledge of better cleaners and understanding of cleaning chemistry greatly improved, but I have even learned to enjoy the creativity of GIY-ing my own cleaners and the empowerment that comes with the control I have over these products.

I've realized how much I love the learning process and what joy comes when some everyday mystery gets explained. One such time I remember distinctly was when I learned that water, as we experience it, is never a neutral pH of 7. This upended one of my most core understandings of chemistry! Every pH scale I've ever seen shows water sitting pretty right in the middle at 7, the epitome of neutrality, neither acidic nor alkaline. But this is only theoretically so. Water as we encounter it is never a 7. It is so chockablock full of ions from various minerals it picks up that the pH swings from 6.5 to 8.5. This explained so much. For one, I learned that pH is tricky business, and that chemistry in action is not nearly as simple as it is in a textbook.

Another positive outcome of my transition to GIY cleaners is that I am completely comfortable with the kids using the cleaning products. This is a huge help to me and, of course, teaches them some valuable life skills. Perhaps they're less thrilled with this development, but nonetheless, I enjoy the peace of mind that comes from knowing they're cleaning the bathroom with the same soap they use to clean themselves.

I have taken liberties with the concept of this chapter because I know The Cleaning Cabinet is not a room unto itself. This space tends to vary from house to house. Whether your cleaning cabinet happens to be in the laundry room like mine or in the garage or in the hallway or in a box you keep at the top of a closet, we are going to stop there and talk about your collection of cleaners.

The best way to know what's in your own cleaners is to make them yourself. While we cannot control all of the chemicals in our houses—ones in textiles and construction materials are particularly oblique—we should take advantage of whatever we can control. Let's get started.

GOING GREEN IN THE CLEANING CABINET

Having confidence in your green cleaners is the first step to adopting them. Soap or detergent and water is all that's needed to keep a house clean, but if you don't think they work, if you don't know how they work, you won't use them. Or you'll use them and then follow them up with chemically burdensome products, just to be sure. That defeats the purpose.

So before we get started with recipes for housecleaning, we're going to have a chemistry lesson.

How Soap Works

Soap cleans by removing dirt, oil, and other debris from a surface. It does this by being both a surfactant and an emulsifier.

The word *surfactant* is a mash up of the phrase "**surf**ace **act**ive a**gent**," which means soap acts against the surface tension of water. Surface tension is a like a skin or membrane at the surface of water made of the attraction of water molecules to one another. It is why some insects can walk on water and why belly flops hurt so very much. Surface tension inhibits cleaning by preventing water from penetrating fully to the grease or grime. The water is too busy holding on to other water molecules. Soap breaks that attraction so the water can get to work.

 LAB COAT MOMENT
Breaking Surface Tension

Let's have some fun with surface tension. Fill a white plate or flat dish with water and sprinkle the top with finely ground pepper. Then dip your finger in soap and lightly touch the center of the water. Observe how the pepper flies to the edges of the dish. The soap breaks the surface tension, which snaps apart like a popped balloon, carrying the pepper with it. You can do this only once with that water. Once the surface tension is broken by even the tiniest bit of soap, it is broken forever. You'll have to rinse out the dish to repeat the demonstration.

The second power of soap is emulsification. An emulsifier blends together two substances that don't want to blend. In this case, we're talking oil and water.

The emulsifying magic of soap lies at the molecular level, where we find something exceedingly rare in chemistry: a molecule that can dissolve in both oil and water. This is because a soap molecule has a polar (or charged) head and a nonpolar (or not charged) tail. The polar head is *hydrophilic*,

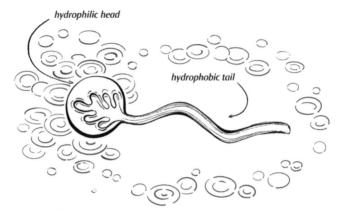

SOAP OR DETERGENT MOLECULE, SIMPLIFIED

hydrophilic head

hydrophobic tail

The two primary components of a soap or detergent molecule are a polar, or charged, head and a nonpolar tail. This difference in charge makes the head hydrophilic, or attracted to water, and the tail lipophilic, or attracted to oil.

from Greek meaning "water loving." The nonpolar tail is *hydrophobic*, or "water fearing," otherwise called *lipophilic*, or "fat loving." Altogether, the soap molecule is *amphiphilic*, which means "lover of both." I find that idea beautiful. If only we all were more amphiphilic.

So the water-loving head dissolves into water and the oil-loving tail dissolves into oil. Soap is a bridge between them. But it's not just one soap molecule per oil molecule. A whole pack of soap molecules—from 50 to 100—surrounds each bit of oil, forming a sphere that encases the oil securely in the middle. This little oil/soap sphere is called a micelle.

The outside of a fully formed micelle is entirely water-loving soap heads, which easily grab hold of passing water molecules and get rinsed away. The rationale behind the 20-second hand-washing recommendation is partially to give the soap time to form into these micelles, and the rinsing action is key to removing the micelles from the skin.

This is how soap cleans. One micelle after another. It does not matter if this process takes place on your skin or on your kitchen counters or on your floor. Soap cleans the same way wherever it is.

A MICELLE

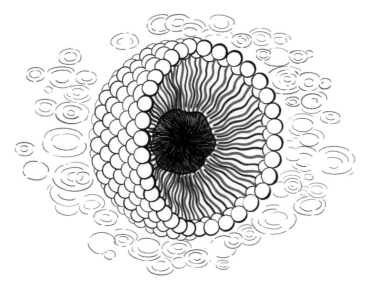

Soap or detergent molecules surround each bit of oil, encasing it in a sphere called a micelle. The lipophilic tails dissolve into the oil, with the hydrophilic heads facing out.

Let me get back to my original statement: soap cleans by removing. It does not primarily clean by killing, though it can inactivate some bacteria and viruses. This ability to remove debris is what makes soap and water more important than antibacterial agents like disinfectants and sanitizers. These latter substances work by killing but do not remove. They leave surfaces (hands, counters) littered with dead microbes. But not all microbes are killed by them. The strongest survive, which is a situation I'll address later with disinfectants. Even when disinfection is recommended, there always is the instruction to first clean the surface with soap and water.[35]

Soap is the first line of defense because it is so good at carrying off everything. It is only clever marketing that has sent the message that soap is not enough.

What's the Difference between Soap and Detergent?

To round out this overview of cleaning chemistry, I have one final note. All this time, I've been talking soap, but not all cleaners are soap. Some are detergents. Detergents are a super vast and diverse assortment. It's hard to generalize about detergents because there are so many, but to try at a very high level, I'll say soaps are simple and detergents are complex. Soaps are made in an easy, one-step reaction, but detergents require multi-step chemical synthesis.

 LAB COAT MOMENT
Emulsification in Action

Let's look at soap's action as both a surfactant and an emulsifier. Fill a plate with milk—we need some fat in the milk for this to work, so use at minimum 2 percent milk, but you could go all the way with heavy cream. Then sprinkle several drops of liquid food coloring on the milk. Don't mix it. Saturate a cotton swab with soap and touch it to the center of the milk. The first thing you will see is the surface tension break. Milk is mostly water and so has surface tension. When the surface tension snaps to the edge, it carries some of the dye with it. That's your first "ooh, aah" moment. But we're not done yet. Keep holding the cotton swab perfectly still at the center of the milk. Don't stir or swirl. If you look closely, you will see that the dye is still moving, slowly, for another 30 seconds or more. What's causing that? You are seeing evidence that the soap molecules are moving throughout the milk, trying to find fat molecules to hide their lipophilic tails in. There are attracting and repelling forces at work here, making the molecules move. The soap tails, attracted to the fat and repelled by the water, will keep moving until they have all connected. As they move, they are bumping into the food coloring, causing it to swirl. I find this mesmerizing.

ORIGIN STORY:
Sal Suds Biodegradable Cleaner

My dad, Jim Bronner, a self-taught chemist who took the mantle of soap-making from his dad, Dr. Bronner, was not one to live with frustration. He was a fixer. One thing that frustrated him was how the Pure-Castile Soap reacted with the minerals in hard water, which we had in hefty doses in Los Angeles and would leave a film of deposits. So, my dad took it upon himself to formulate a cleanser that would not react with hard water, which meant it would have to be a detergent, with its more durable molecular structure. Even so, it would still be very mild, biodegradable, made from plant-based oils, tough on stains, and exceptionally clean rinsing. Thus, Sal Suds was born.

Analyzing soaps versus detergents is not a question of good versus bad. There certainly can be poorly formulated soaps with super high pH that would be very damaging to skin, just as there are super bad detergents that are damaging to both body and environment. However, there are also mild soaps and mild detergents that are well crafted. Let me introduce you to the detergent that Dr. Bronner's makes: Sal Suds Biodegradable Cleaner. Everything I said above about soap being a surfactant and an emulsifier is true of Sal Suds as well.

Scented in its original version with Siberian fir needle and white spruce essential oils, Sal Suds is free of synthetic fragrance and dyes. And it's highly concentrated. Just a tiny amount of Sal Suds will do for most situations, and indeed I use it for most situations. Laundry, dishes, floors, cars, bathrooms, kitchens. If it needs to be washed, I wash it with Sal Suds. My life would be so much harder without it.

There is a lot of overlap in the uses of Sal Suds and the Pure-Castile Soap. Let me answer that question next.

Sal Suds or Pure-Castile Soap: Which to Use When

Both the Pure-Castile and Sal Suds are exceedingly, exceedingly versatile and many times interchangeable. But not always.

The Pure-Castile Soap is designed first and foremost for the body. The blend of oils (coconut, olive, palm or palm kernel, jojoba, and hempseed) is the most nourishing to our skin. However, because it is such a beautifully simple soap, it can clean so much more amazingly well, whether it's your dog, your sinks, or your floors.

The one drawback to the Pure-Castile Soap, as I mentioned in the Sal Suds origin, is that as a true soap, it reacts with the minerals in hard water, forming an insoluble (meaning "doesn't dissolve") residue. This residue is harmless, but there are a few places where it is particularly undesirable: it leaves an unsightly film on shiny surfaces like cars and glassware and can reduce the absorbency of fabrics, such as towels, athletic wear, and diapers.

There are easy remedies for these situations, which I'll discuss later on, but to avoid the residues altogether, we have Sal Suds.

Because Sal Suds is a detergent, it has an inherently more stable molecule that does not react with hard water and runs no risk of leaving films on shiny or absorbent surfaces. Plus, Sal Suds is even more concentrated than the Pure-Castile Soap, so you use less at a time, making your bottle last longer. And finally, Sal Suds is tougher on stains.

That still leaves a lot of overlap where either of the cleansers will work, except for these few situations:

Situations where I exclusively use Pure-Castile Soap:
+ On people
+ On animals
+ On plants

Situations where I exclusively use Sal Suds:
+ Cars

✦ Down and down alternative items like comforters, sleeping bags, and jackets

✦ On and around outdoor surfaces like decks and siding

✦ Shiny or clear surfaces that might show hard water deposits

Beyond performance, there are several considerations that might influence your preference. While both are certified vegan, the Pure-Castile Soap is made with certified organic oils. The Sal Suds is more concentrated and therefore is more budget-friendly.

RECIPES AND HOW-TOS

Now you know how soap works. You know some helpful vocabulary. You even learned some Greek. You're ready to make your own housecleaning solutions and take control over the chemistry in your house. This is where it gets simple.

GIY ALL-PURPOSE CLEANING SPRAY

In the first chapter, I said there were two dilutions I wanted you to put this book down right now and go make. The first was the Foaming Hand Soap (page 45). The second is this: GIY All-Purpose Cleaning Spray. This is the foundation of my housecleaning arsenal. Conventional all-purpose sprays contain excessively aggressive cleaners that are not only unnecessary but also harmful to the user and bystanders, plus they leave residues or fragrances. And they cost more.

1 quart (1 L) water

¼ cup (60 ml) Pure-Castile Liquid Soap OR 1 tablespoon (15 ml) Sal Suds Biodegradable Cleaner OR ½ cup (120 ml) Soap Cream (see page 160)

20 drops tea tree essential oil (optional)

HOW TO:

1. Fill a spray bottle with the water first. (The order is important here because if you put the water in second, you'll get an overflow of bubbles. It's messy.)

2. Add the Pure-Castile Soap or Sal Suds and the tea tree essential oil, if desired. Swirl gently to mix.

3. Spray surfaces and wipe with a damp cloth. Alternatively, spray a damp cloth and wipe surfaces. The dampness in the cloth is important because it is this water that the soap will latch on to for rinsing. If you spray and wipe with a dry cloth, you'll leave soap behind.

WHAT KIND OF WATER: In general tap water is fine. However, if your tap water is hard, the Pure-Castile Soap will cause a cloudy precipitate to settle on the bottom of the spray bottle. This is completely harmless and does not mean the solution is contaminated or won't work. But if this bothers you, you can get a clear solution by using distilled or filtered water. Or use Sal Suds.

TEA TREE ESSENTIAL OIL: I list it here because it can help make the transition away from conventional cleaners. It adds a convincingly clean scent, and the research about tea tree essential oil's antimicrobial properties is bountiful.[36] It gives this solution an extra antimicrobial punch. Oftentimes, when I'm doing general cleaning, I don't add it because I am very confident in the cleaning power of the Pure-Castile Soap and Sal Suds. However, in times of particular illness or for anyone having trouble letting go of a conventional cleaner, it's reassuring to add.

ANT SPRAY

I discovered this use for the GIY All-Purpose Cleaning Spray by accident years back. One day to my horror, I realized that the flecks of black in my kitchen countertop were moving. They were ants. In desperation I grabbed the GIY All-Purpose Cleaning Spray that was nearby and found that it stopped them on contact. I've since learned that soap is an approved insecticide under the USDA's National Organic Program and that tea tree essential oil erases the scent markings ants leave behind so others can't follow. So I'm cleaning my counters and eliminating ants at the same time.

SCOURING POWDER

This replaces any sort of powdered cleaner you may be using. It is cheaper and just as effective. I use scouring powder on all sinks, tubs, toilets, grout, ovens—anything that has a buildup of gunk. This is so simple and really makes things sparkle.

Baking soda

Optional for scent: 10 drops essential oil per cup of baking soda

HOW TO:

1. This isn't so much a recipe as just an instruction. Fill a shaker jar with baking soda. You can stop right there if you want and be done with it.

2. However, if you want to be fancy, put your baking soda in a bowl and sprinkle on the essential oil. Toss it with a fork until blended. Put it in the shaker jar.

3. To use, spray the surface with the GIY All-Purpose Cleaning Spray and then sprinkle on the scouring powder. Scrub with a stiff brush and rinse.

GLASS CLEANING

Here's another super simple combination. It almost feels like cheating. This glass cleaner is a great "first step" in green cleaning, if the whole Green-It-Yourself idea is sounding a little daunting. Conventional glass cleaner isn't the worst offender, but if you can do it this simply and cheaply, why make it more complicated?

1 part vinegar

1 part water

HOW TO:

1. Combine in a spray bottle.

2. Spray glass surfaces—mirrors, shower doors, windows—and wipe with a lint-free cloth or squeegee.

ALTERNATIVE GLASS CLEANER: Pure club soda. This works just as well as vinegar and water. I list it as the alternative because it's a little less handy. And the club soda works best when it's fresh and fizzy, so it doesn't have the best shelf life.

MOPPING: TILE, STONE, WOOD, VINYL, LAMINATE

I once asked my readers what tools they used to mop their floors. I got 168 different techniques, including a string mop, a flat head mop, microfiber head, a steam mop, a self-propelled mop, a spinning mop, a brush, and a rag. For holding the cleaning solution, there were buckets, spray bottles, squirt bottles, sinks. Whatever you use, here's the solution to put in it. (My math-y folks out there may notice that these two are the same ratio, differing in their volume.)

FOR A BUCKET, SINK, OR OTHER LARGE DUNKING VESSEL:

1 gallon (4 L) water (see Note)

3 tablespoons (45 ml) Pure-Castile Soap OR ½ teaspoon (2.5 ml) Sal Suds

FOR A SPRAY BOTTLE, SQUIRT BOTTLE, OR SIMILAR HANDHELD CONTAINER:

1 quart (1 L) water

2 teaspoons (10 ml) Pure-Castile Soap OR ⅛ teaspoon Sal Suds (0.6 ml)

HOW TO:

1. Add the water to the bucket or bottle first, and then add the Pure-Castile Soap or Sal Suds. This reduces bubbling and overflow.

2. With the bucket, submerge the mophead in the bucket and then wring nearly dry before mopping. With the squirt bottle, use a damp mop, and squirt either the floor or the mophead with the solution before mopping. No need to rinse.

NOTE: I do realize that 4 L is 215 ml shy of 1 gallon, and 1 L is 54 ml shy of a quart. However, for these dilutions, the ease of measuring trumps the exactness, and you are always welcome to fiddle with the dilutions to your liking. The only issue with using more Pure-Castile Soap or Sal Suds than listed is that you'll end up with extra bubbles to clean up.

GIY SOFT SCRUB

Karen Logan's excellent Earth Scrub recipe from her book, Clean House, Clean Planet, *inspired this recipe. I enjoy making this one with the kids. It is the beauty of chemistry at work, and it creates a supremely useful solution that is so much cheaper than conventional scrubs, plus leaves out any bleach or other harmful ingredients.*

1 cup (240 ml) Pure-Castile Soap OR ¼ cup (60 ml) Sal Suds
3⅓ cups (800 g) baking soda
1 cup (240 ml) water
¼ cup (60 ml) white vinegar

HOW TO:

1. In a big bowl, combine the baking soda with the Pure-Castile Soap or the Sal Suds. Mix it with a fork until well-blended and no lumps remain.

2. Add in the water and mix thoroughly again. Add in the vinegar and keep stirring until no lumps remain. (Read my explanation below

for why vinegar and the Pure-Castile or Sal Suds are OK in this combination.) Add additional water if needed until the mixture is a pourable consistency.

3. Use a funnel to pour the solution into an empty quart bottle. This mixture will thicken if left to sit for several weeks. If you find a white solid at the bottom, add a few more tablespoons of vinegar and swirl to mix.

4. To use, squirt the GIY Soft Scrub over the surface and wipe or scrub with a cloth or brush. Rinse with a wet cloth.

TOILET CLEANING

Again, this is not so much a recipe as a method. Each of the cleaners I list here is used above. There is no need to make a specific toilet-cleaning solution, given that the same blends of soap and water do the cleaning.

If your toilet is extra grimy, you'll get the best cleaning impact if you empty the bowl of water. This way the cleaners can sit on the surface for longer and have more impact. To do this, turn off the water to the toilet bowl by closing the valve at the wall behind it. Then empty the bowl by flushing it.

I have three different methods for GIY cleaning a toilet. I switch between these three constantly.

METHOD 1:

Spray the bowl thoroughly with the GIY All-Purpose Cleaning Spray and brush with a toilet brush. This works best if you've been regularly cleaning your toilet and the grime isn't built up.

METHOD 2:

Take it up a notch. Squirt a very small amount (approximately ½ teaspoon or 2.5 ml) of the undiluted Pure-Castile Soap or an even smaller amount (3 drops) of the Sal Suds directly onto the toilet bowl brush. Brush the bowl thoroughly.

BOOST FOR METHODS 1 OR 2: For extra scrubbing action, sprinkle baking soda onto your toilet brush before scrubbing.

METHOD 3:

For the deepest clean, use the GIY Soft Scrub. Squirt the scrub around the bowl, and brush well.

Whichever method you choose, it is important to let it sit for about 10 minutes for maximum effectiveness. Then give the bowl a final scrub, turn the water back on if you turned it off, and flush.

GIY HOUSECLEANING WIPES

The convenience of wipes is nice—cleaner and cloth in one handy package. Here's how to make your own.

For Reusable Wipes: *Cut some old soft cotton T-shirts into wipe-sized squares that can be washed after each use.*

For Disposable Wipes: *Cut a paper towel roll cut in half (an electric knife works best).*

SOLUTION
   1½ cup (360 ml) water
   1 tablespoon (15 ml) Pure-Castile Liquid Soap OR ½ tablespoon
      (7.5 ml) Sal Suds
   ¼ teaspoon (20 drops) tea tree essential oil
   Closable container large enough to hold the wipes

Combine the solution ingredients in a jar and swirl gently to mix. Then place the wipes in the container. For disposable wipes, place the cut roll upright on its end. Reusable wipes can be placed in any direction. Pour the solution over the wipes. Cover the container and let sit 20 minutes or until the wipes soak up all the liquid. At this point with the disposable wipes, you will be able to pull the cardboard tube out of the center, and then the wipes will dispense easily from the middle. Use the wipes around your house or pack them up in a sealable bag for on-the-go use. These have a shelf-life of 1 to 2 weeks.

Hard Water and Soap

Several times now I have alluded to hard water. Water is termed "hard" when it contains a high concentration of minerals like calcium and magnesium. Soft water has a low concentration of calcium and magnesium ions. Areas with higher annual rainfall tend to have softer water. You can find out if you have hard or soft water in the Lab Coat Moment below.

Hard water can be artificially softened at home with an ion exchanger, which swaps sodium and potassium ions for the calcium and magnesium. Minerals can also be removed from hard water by filtration or distillation.

Soft versus hard water sounds like a case of good versus bad, but it's not that simple. Soft water lathers soap better and uses less soap to clean. However, in artificially softened water, soap may have trouble fully rinsing off of skin because the sodium and potassium ions in the water slightly repel soap. You may rinse your hands and then find you can still re-lather them.

Hard water, however, has its own set of difficulties. While it provides essential minerals in calcium and magnesium, hard water can be drying to skin and hair and exacerbate eczema. The harder the water, the more drying and exacerbating it can be. Hard water also leaves calcium deposits, commonly called scale, on fixtures. When hard water mixes with soap, it forms a residue on bathroom surfaces and fabrics. It is this last substance which we now have to tackle here in the cleaning cabinet.

LAB COAT MOMENT
Testing for Water Hardness

Test your home water for hardness by filling a clear glass with tap water and adding a few drops of a true soap like Dr. Bronner's Pure-Castile Liquid Soap. If the soap produces a cloudy swirl as it makes its way through the water, it is reacting with calcium and magnesium ions, indicating that the water is hard. If the soap remains clear as it swirls through the water, then the water is soft. There are more precise testing kits that can tell you an exact hardness level, but this quick soap test gives you a general idea.

What Is Soap Scum?

Soap scum is not unrinsed soap. Instead it is a residue formed from the reaction between the minerals in hard water and soap. This reaction forms a film that adheres to bathroom fixtures and fabrics and does not dissolve in water on its own.

HOW TO GET RID OF SOAP SCUM

METHOD 1: DISSOLVE IT

While these residues are insoluble in water, they do dissolve in acid. Therefore, the acetic acid of vinegar is a great tool for lifting these deposits off of surfaces and fabrics.

1 cup (240 ml) white vinegar
1 quart (1 L) water

Combine the vinegar and water in a spray bottle and spray on surfaces. Let sit for about 5 minutes (*not long enough for it to dry*), and then rinse it away with very hot water. If the buildup is particularly thick, you may have to repeat this process. *Do not use this method on soft stones like marble or travertine; the acidity can etch the surface.*

For laundry that has been washed with Pure-Castile Soap, add vinegar to the fabric softener compartment so that it releases during the rinse cycle: ½ cup (120 ml) for a large high-efficiency (HE) load and 1 cup (240 ml) for a standard washer.

METHOD 2: SCOUR IT

This uses the mechanical action of a scouring powder, namely baking soda. Spray surface with GIY All-Purpose Cleaning Spray and then sprinkle with baking soda. Scrub surfaces with a cloth or brush and rinse with hot water. Again, be careful not to use too stiff a brush with soft stones. This is the method I use the most. It's very fast.

METHOD 3: SOFT-SCRUB IT

I love this method if I've taken the time to make up a batch of GIY Soft Scrub. Squirt the GIY Soft Scrub on surfaces and scrub with a cloth or brush. Rinse well with hot water.

Lastly, after whichever method, dry the surfaces thoroughly.

HOW TO PREVENT MINERAL DEPOSITS

Better than being able to get rid of the deposits is not having them in the first place. Here are a few ideas to remain in that happy sparkly state:

1. Consider a whole-house or point-of-use water softener, weighing the benefits and drawbacks.

2. After bathing, squeegee or towel residual water off surfaces, especially glass shower doors.

3. Clean your bathroom regularly. This prevents the buildup. A small amount of residue is much easier to remove when there isn't that much of it. To state the obvious.

4. At the end of your shower, spray the walls with diluted vinegar (only if they're not soft stone like marble or travertine) and then rinse them down with water.

Is There Residue on Me, Too?

We do not find these deposits on our skin for a few reasons. When we towel off, the towel absorbs potential deposits. Plus, our skin constantly excretes sebum, an oily substance that is slightly acidic, and as I mentioned, acids dissolve these residues.

Water Spots and Scale

The minerals in hard water alone, even when they don't interact with soap, can leave deposits that are noticeable on shiny surfaces like glass and metal. We call these small mineral deposits "water spots," or when they've built up significantly to a whiteish crust, we call it "scale." To prevent these, dry surfaces fully with a towel or squeegee. Drinking glasses, stainless steel appliances, showerheads, glass shower doors, windows, mirrors. If you already have water spots and scale, an acid is the easiest way to remove them. Take the vinegar dilution you used before and spray them, or spray a cloth and wipe them down. For significant scale on a showerhead or a faucet, soak a washcloth in the vinegar solution and then rubber band it around the showerhead along with a plastic bag for 10 minutes. Remove it and dry the showerhead with a towel. Repeated exposure to acid can etch metals, so it is best to prevent the scale rather than repeatedly clean it with vinegar.

Green Cleaners That Don't Come in a Bottle

Heat

Heat plays an important role in effective green cleaning. Hot water helps loosen the hold grime can have on surfaces, be it dishes, floors, or fabrics. While only extreme heat can kill microbes (think autoclave), hot water (around 130°F/55°C) loosens grime and boosts the cleaning ability and speed of a soap. Use heat judiciously because there is a cost to it. Not only does it cost energy to heat the water, but heat can also degrade fabrics faster and depletes our skin of oils. Here are some ways to employ heat in your cleaning:

✦ Dip a dishcloth in hot water, or briefly microwave a damp dishcloth, before tackling countertops and stainless steel appliances.
✦ Mop with hot water.
✦ Steam mops are a chemical-free way to loosen grime on tile floors.
✦ Washing laundry on hot can loosen more grime from fabrics.
✦ Hot dryers can deactivate microbes as well as mites.
✦ Boiling water poured from a kettle can also kill small weeds in your driveway or patio.
✦ Self-cleaning ovens clean with extreme heat.

NOTE: Always take care when using heat and steam, so as not to burn yourself.

Time

When it comes to cleaning, time is your friend. The longer any cleaner is in contact with a surface, the more effectively it will clean. Remember this for icky surfaces: meaty cutting boards or toilets. Spray with the GIY All-Purpose Cleaning Spray, scrub it, then let it sit for 10 minutes before wiping or rinsing it off.

Time also helps with surfaces that are hard to clean with sprays and cloths. Because most microbes die within a day or two, if you isolate a surface, eventually the germs will die. Time does not remove dirt, grime, or dead germs, but it can still be a tool for a successful cleaning regimen.

Sunlight

The UV rays of the sun aid both disinfecting and bleaching. While not enough alone to clean, sunlight gives an extra boost of clean to an object like a wooden cutting board if you put it directly in the sun and is a great tool for whitening and brightening white fabrics. Sunlight is a low-energy way to dry your laundry. Rooms that are exposed to sunlight have lower bacterial counts.[37] So let the sun shine in!

Fresh Air

I cannot overstate the importance of fresh air for a clean home that promotes our personal health. We focus so much of our energy on cleaning surfaces, but it is the air itself with which we come into the greatest and most constant contact. In the name of efficiency, our homes are sealed tight so as not to lose heated or cooled air. The downside has been that our indoor air pollution levels have increased, often making our indoor air more polluted than outdoor air.[38] Fortunately, the solution here is simple: open your windows. Flush out the air. When that is not possible, use air purifiers, whole house fans, exhaust fans, and in dry climates set HVAC fans to "On" instead of "Auto" to circulate air through filters. (This is not advisable in humid climates because running the HVAC without the compressor can increase indoor humidity levels and contribute to mold formation.)

HOW CLEAN IS CLEAN? OR WHY DISINFECTANTS AT HOME ARE MOSTLY UNNECESSARY

Clean, sanitize, disinfect, sterilize. While these terms may seem like synonyms and we may use them interchangeably, these words have distinctive meanings. The word *clean* means the *removal* of all manner of material from a surface and applies to the widest range of contaminants by the use of soap or detergent. The remaining three are various degrees of *killing* living microbes and are not regularly called for in household situations. When they are, cleaning always precedes any of the other methods so that debris doesn't interfere with the ability of the more intensive agents to access microbes. None of the killing means are effective without the step of cleaning first.

As with much in this world, managing dirt and germs is an exercise in balancing risks and benefits. The benefits of cleaning, and the fundamental reasons we do it, involve promoting and protecting health and improving appearance.

The risks of excessive cleaning are that we may expose ourselves to harmful substances and can promote antimicrobial resistance. When we move to more intense cleaning agents, we increase these risks. We need to be sure the benefit merits that risk, only increasing the intensity of our cleaners in times of sickness or vulnerability. Healthy people interacting in everyday circumstances do not benefit from intense sanitizing or disinfecting and may create the situations they intend to prevent.

What Is Antimicrobial Resistance?

The World Health Organization (WHO) has declared antimicrobial resistance to be one of the top 10 global health threats facing humanity.[39] Antimicrobial resistance describes cases in which microbes (bacteria, viruses, fungi) are no longer susceptible to the agents we've heretofore relied upon to control them, resulting in the wider spread of disease, serious illness, and death.

Numerous studies have found that the frequent use of disinfectants increases the likelihood of resistance and have concluded that disinfectants should be reserved for circumstances in which their impact is essential and proven.[40] Further, in addition to overuse, studies show that the misuse of disinfectants promotes resistance, whether it's using them below the instructed concentration or using them for less than the instructed time.[41] Frequent and unmerited use of disinfectants at home, including the commonly used chlorine and alcohol disinfectants, have been identified as sources of developing resistance.[42]

In summary, disinfectants at home should not be used regularly and should be reserved for targeted circumstances. When they are used, be sure to adhere strictly to the instructions for exposure volume and duration. Refer to the EPA's Safer Choice lists for disinfectants. Cleaning with soap or detergent and water, plus fresh air, is all that's needed at home on a regular basis.

Changing the Smell of Clean

Smell can be the biggest obstacle in changing any habit, including the conversion to a different way of cleaning. Our emotional attachment to scents and the connections we make with them are powerful. There is a neurological reason for this. In our brain, scent, emotion, and memory are all wrapped up together. Often, the way we judge whether something is clean is not to look closely for dirt but to see how it smells. For example, if we have long associated the smell of diluted bleach with the impression that a bathroom is clean, it can be a challenge to break that connection.

Green cleaners don't smell the same as conventional. They don't have that nose-scouring pungency or even that one particular scent a person has long associated with "clean."

However, it is these very smells that are the problems. The worst sources of these smells are volatile organic compounds (VOCs). VOCs are molecules of the substances themselves in the air. Let me put it this way: it is not a *scent* of bleach in your nose and lungs—it *is* bleach in your nose and lungs. You know how powerful bleach is on your toilet? It's just as powerful in your lungs, but your lungs aren't built to withstand it. This is what makes VOCs so bad.

The other problematic source for the smell of cleaners is, of course, fragrance. The hazards of fragrance in housecleaning products are the same as in personal care—allergens, sensitizers, endocrine disruptors, carcinogens—but often in much higher doses. Certain cleaning products—laundry products come most to mind—promise to leave a lingering scent for days or longer. This lingering scent means there is a residue left behind, indicating that the surface is not actually clean. Further, the compounds that make those fragrances so enduring on surfaces also make them very enduring in our bodies when we breathe them in. VOCs and fragrance are a primary source of indoor air pollution and a frequent asthma trigger.

In switching to green cleaners, redefining the smell of clean can be an opportunity for a lot of fun. Revel in the freedom. When you make your own cleaners, you can make them smell however you want by blending essential oils. Start with just a few drops in your GIY solutions—these pack a punch and a little goes a long way. If you are particularly missing the pungency of a conventional cleaner, give tea tree essential oil a try.

Blending it with eucalyptus makes a cleanest of clean scent. Also remember that if something is truly clean, if there truly is nothing on the surface, then it smells like nothing at all.

Worst Offenders among Conventional Housecleaners

POWERFUL SOLVENTS: Two household cleaners are designed to eat through solid objects. This makes them the most dangerous cleaners for accidental skin contact and exceptionally dangerous if ingested. I speak of drain cleaners and oven cleaners that contain sodium hydroxide, potassium hydroxide, or sulfuric acid. Not only do they pose great risk due to accidental exposure, but they can also corrode pipes and oven surfaces and are environmentally catastrophic downstream.

Please evict these from your house and dispose of them at your nearest hazardous waste disposal center. Clear drains instead with plumbing snakes, by opening the P-trap, or by calling a plumber. A flush of very hot water may also do the trick. See my oven cleaning methods in The Kitchen.

BLEACH: Although "bleach" is a generic term for a substance that removes color, here I mean sodium hypochlorite, which is the standard substance we call household bleach. I was stunned to learn that people who clean regularly, either for a living or their own homes, are 30 percent more likely to have Chronic Obstructive Pulmonary Disease (COPD) due to bleach. This is the impact of VOCs on our lungs. That meant me. I was the primary cleaner of my house. Cleaning should improve our lives, not worsen them. Both bleach and quaternium compounds were cited as causes in this 30-year study. There are other ways to clean and whiten. Read more about the downsides of bleach in The Laundry Room.

Avoid These Oft-Recommended Green Cleaning Combinations

There is some bad green cleaning advice out there. People mean well, but they forget what I've already told you: chemistry happens. Two cleaners may be great on their own but not when they're put together.

Castile Soap (or Any True Soap) and Vinegar (or Any Acid)

I've been trying to bust this green cleaning myth since the earliest days of my blogging. In most cases, castile soap and vinegar should not be combined. This is a fundamental acid/base reaction. Yes, pH again. It is not dangerous, but it is completely pointless. Vinegar is an acid, with a pH around 3. Soap is an alkali. Soap is always an alkali. Dr. Bronner's Pure-Castile Soap has a pH around 9.2. When this acid and alkali get together, they break each other down. What's left are free fatty acids (read "oils") that will not clean any surface.

I know I am spoiling so many recipes in saying this, but please hear me. This does not work. Not if you use hot water, not if you swirl it, not if you add other ingredients (exception below with GIY Soft Scrub). If you add a lot more soap than vinegar, there will be unreacted soap to do some cleaning. If you add more vinegar than soap, there will be unreacted vinegar to lift some grease, but you are wasting all the soap that reacts with the vinegar. Use one or the other but not both together.

LAB COAT MOMENT
Soap + Vinegar = Gunk

See this reaction for yourself. Coat your fingers in a couple drops of olive oil and then wash them with soap and water. Observe if the soap and water remove the oil. Then, in a small dish, combine castile soap and vinegar. It will turn milky white and chunky. Then coat your fingers again in a couple drops of olive oil. Wash them in the soap/vinegar combo. Which combination gets the oil off your skin better? Which combination will get grime off your household surfaces better?

Baking Soda and Vinegar

In for a penny, in for a pound. I may as well get the rest of the green cleaning establishment upset with me. If you search online for a green oven cleaner or green drain cleaner, you will get pagefuls of recommendations that combining baking soda and vinegar will make a cleaning agent. Don't believe it.

I know what you're thinking. "But it's so fizzy! Surely it's working!" There is an acid/base reaction happening, but it does not have cleaning power. Baking soda (or sodium bicarbonate) and vinegar (acetic acid) react and form three substances: carbon dioxide, sodium acetate, and water. The carbon dioxide makes that satisfying fizz as it bubbles away, but carbon dioxide isn't a cleaning agent. Sodium acetate, which is the sodium salt of acetic acid, has uses—such as acting as a buffer against further changes in pH and in food, medicine, and concrete manufacturing—but it does not clean. And then there's water.

Functionally, the water is the best cleaner of the three substances here. If your surface happens to be cleaner after this reaction, it is likely the water and whatever you wiped it up with that did it. You would have done better to use the baking soda and water alone. Add some soap for extra cleaning.

I've read the testimonials that insist this reaction cleared a drain. They loaded the drain with baking soda, added vinegar, and then followed it with a gallon of hot water. You know what did the work? The hot water. Baking soda and vinegar? All fizz, no function.

Dangerous Cleaning Combinations

While the abovementioned combos are ineffective but harmless, the combinations that follow are dangerous and even deadly. I mention them because someone might combine them with the best of intentions, thinking that two cleaners separately would produce a great cleaner together. That's not how it works. Say it with me now: chemistry happens.

+ Bleach and ammonia—produce mustard gas
+ Bleach and vinegar—produce chlorine gas
+ Bleach and rubbing alcohol—produce chloroform
+ Hydrogen peroxide and vinegar—produce peracetic acid

In summary, never mix anything with chlorine bleach. As dangerous as bleach is on its own, it can be worse. If you have any store-bought cleaners with multiple ingredients, don't mix them. You might not realize that the ingredients include some of the above. Don't mix a store-bought cleaner with what you perceive as a green cleaner without doing some research.

Ask Lisa

Q You emphasize not to mix vinegar with Pure-Castile Soap or Sal Suds, but the GIY Soft Scrub recipe has both. Why is it OK here?

A I love chemistry questions! Short answer: the baking soda acts as a buffer, or protector, between the vinegar and the Pure-Castile Soap or Sal Suds. Vinegar reacts more readily with baking soda than it does with either cleaner. The astute reader will also comment that I said above that vinegar and baking soda do not make an effective cleaning combination. That is still true. The purpose of their reaction here is not to boost the cleaning efficacy, but rather to create the structure of the GIY Soft Scrub. The reaction produces carbon dioxide gas, which gets trapped by the soap or Sal Suds in bubbles, creating the lovely foamy texture that enables the scrub to cling to vertical surfaces.

Q I already combined the soap and the vinegar and now I have a mess! How do I clean it up?

A Since the gunk is made of released fatty acids, or oils, clean it up with soap. Plain soap. If you still have Dr. Bronner's on hand, use either the Pure-Castile Soap or the Sal Suds. Sal Suds is a bit better at picking up oils, so if you have a choice, go with that.

Q Is vinegar a disinfectant? Can I clean my whole house with vinegar?

A While vinegar is effective against some microbes, it is not effective against enough of them to be a reliable disinfectant. As a general cleaner, vinegar is effective at dissolving the minerals in water spots and can lift light amounts of grease but is not effective at removing other dirt and debris on surfaces. Plus, the acidity of vinegar can etch, dull, or corrode certain surfaces, such as soft stones, wood, and certain metals, over time. While vinegar has a definite place in the green cleaning arsenal, it is not sufficient on its own.

Q Are Dr. Bronner's Pure-Castile Soap and Sal Suds antibacterial?

A No. In order to be antibacterial, a product must contain a pesticidal ingredient that broadly kills microbes. Neither Sal Suds nor the Pure-Castile Soap contain such an ingredient. They clean by removing, not by killing.

Q I notice that Sal Suds contains sodium lauryl sulfate. Isn't that a really bad ingredient?

A Sodium lauryl sulfate (SLS) has been the scapegoat for a mountain of misdirected antipathy over the past several decades. I can't think of another surfactant that has generated so much misplaced wrath, happily whipped to a frenzy by calculating marketers all too willing to take advantage of paranoia. It has been accused of being everything from a neurotoxin to a carcinogen. The only thing it is guilty of is being too good at its job. SLS is a surfactant that is incredibly good at picking up oils. Because of this, it makes a superb degreaser for dishes and laundry and even automotive cleanup.

However, this is not a great trait when it comes to skin care. It grabs too many oils out of our skin, leaving skin depleted and irritated. SLS should not be in body care products, though it is ubiquitous in toothpastes and shampoos and other bubbly products. Other than being an irritant, it does not pose harm to humans. However, it is often guilty by association of problems with sodium laureth sulfate. That one little "-eth" syllable indicates the ingredient underwent ethoxylation, a process that produces the potentially carcinogenic by-product 1,4-dioxane.

Q Can I mix Pure-Castile Soap with . . .? (Cleaning Cabinet Edition)

A Back in The Bathroom, I gave you a list of things people have asked me about mixing into the Pure-Castile Soap to put on their bodies. Here's the housecleaning counterpart. All of these are from questions I've received. If you don't see the mix-in you're wondering about, check The Bathroom chart. What's the principle to remember? Chemistry happens.

continues

Ingredient Combinations with Dr. Bronner's Pure-Castile Soap and Sal Suds

MIX OPTION	INTENT	USE WITH PURE-CASTILE AND SAL SUDS?	ELABORATION
Baking soda	To create a scrubbing cleanser	Yes	Baking soda adds a soft abrasion to the cleaning power of Pure-Castile Soap and Sal Suds. This makes a good scrubber for grimy sinks and fabrics. In laundry, it is a whitener and deodorizer.
Chlorine bleach (aka sodium hypochlorite)	To remove stains and whiten fabrics	No	If you're cleaning with the Pure-Castile Soap or Sal Suds in an effort to be safer, you're undoing that effort by adding bleach.
Borax	To boost surface and laundry cleaning	Yes	Borax does not react with the Pure-Castile Soap or Sal Suds. See my discussion of borax in The Laundry Room before using it.
Pure-Castile Soap	To create a customized scent	Yes	Combining two different Pure-Castile Soap scents is a fantastic way to achieve your perfect blend. Combining the Pure-Castile Soap with Sal Suds is not reactive, but I don't see the point. If it's the scent of the Pure-Castile Soap that's desired plus the stain-fighting power of the Sal Suds, I recommend using essential oils with the Sal Suds.
Essential oils	To create a customized scent	Yes	This can make green cleaning even more fun! Start with just a few drops of essential oils and increase as preferred. Look for organic pure essential oils.

MIX OPTION	INTENT	USE WITH PURE-CASTILE AND SAL SUDS?	ELABORATION
Hydrogen peroxide (H_2O_2)	To remove stains and whiten fabrics	No	Hydrogen peroxide is listed on the EPA's Safer Chemicals Ingredient List as a safer antimicrobial and an oxidant. When mixed with the Pure-Castile Soap or Sal Suds, hydrogen peroxide quickly doffs its extra oxygen, becoming mere H_2O, more commonly known as water. Functionally, this is a fancy and pointless way of diluting with water.
Lemon juice	To boost cleaning	No	Lemon juice is an excellent addition to your green cleaning toolbox but, like vinegar, not a good partner for soap or Sal Suds. Lemon juice is not shelf stable. Left at room temperature it will ferment and outgas. In a closed bottle, it will explode.
Lemon oil (and other citrus oils)	To customize scent	Yes	I am specifically calling out lemon essential oil, in addition to my general statement about essential oils, because of the confusion I've heard from readers over why lemon oil is OK to mix in but lemon juice is not. Lemon juice is an acidic, water-based liquid extracted from the pulp of the fruit. Lemon oil is extracted from the rind of fruit. Oils do not have a pH, which is a measurement only of water-based solutions.

MIX OPTION	INTENT	USE WITH PURE-CASTILE AND SAL SUDS?	ELABORATION
Oxygen bleach	To fight stains	No	Oxygen bleach is most effective against stains when dissolved alone in water as a presoak. Mixing it with soap or detergent accelerates the destabilizing of hydrogen peroxide, leaving mere washing soda behind.
Ethanol or isopropyl alcohol (including any drinking alcohol)	To add disinfecting capabilities	No	Alcohol is an antiseptic and disinfectant listed on the EPA's short list of safer antimicrobial cleaners. Alcohol reduces the foaming of a surfactant and, at higher concentrations, impedes its cleaning ability. Rather than combining the disinfectant with soap, the WHO and the CDC recommend a two-step method: wash surfaces with the GIY All-Purpose Cleaning Spray and then treat with the alcohol. See "How Clean Is Clean" on page 103 for use of disinfectants.
Vinegar	To boost cleaning	No	Not only does vinegar unsaponify soap, it also reduces Sal Suds' cleaning ability.
Washing soda	To boost laundry cleaning	Yes	While there is no reaction between washing soda—aka sodium carbonate—and the Pure-Castile Soap or Sal Suds, see the discussion in The Laundry Room before using it.

CHAPTER 3

THE LAUNDRY ROOM

"Asking for help isn't giving up," said the horse. "It's refusing to give up."
—**CHARLIE MACKESY**

There's a story my Uncle Ralph (my father's older brother) would tell about my grandfather Dr. Bronner and a woman who called him one day.

My grandfather printed his personal phone number on each of his soap bottles. It rang directly into his living room. The woman on the other end of the line had been in despair, at a loss for where to turn. In the midst of her crisis, her eyes fell on a strange text-encrusted soap bottle sitting on her bathroom sink whereon she noticed a phone number, which she called.

My grandfather answered as he always did, listened briefly to her situation, and advised her, "Clean your house and call me back!" She did both, and then they talked for hours. She said her life was transformed.

There is much that I pull from this account. How important one conversation can be. How valuable the connection to one human voice. How much we never know the impact we might have on a stranger. But looking at the specifics of my grandfather's first advice to her, where of all he could have started to address her despair, he began with, "Clean your house." In other words, find something to take control of, remind yourself that you indeed still have power and strength and ability. Raise your eyes and see what's around you. Move in it. Improve it. Then you'll be ready to tackle the bigger crisis inside you.

This is also a powerful lesson in how our physical surroundings have a role to play in our mental, emotional, and spiritual well-being. There is something deeply therapeutic about physical busyness and about cleaning in particular. There's order, renewal, and accomplishment that come from organizing or beautifying what is before us that boosts a feeling of competence and even self-worth within us. Gaining control over physical spaces sparks confidence that control over intangible spaces is possible, too.

And so, whenever I am frustrated, anxious, or upset, one of my best strategies is to do a little busy something: tidy, cook, exercise, crochet, garden, launder, iron. A little physical task that gives my mind and heart time to settle and provides a visible reminder that, despite the current hurdle, I can still affect and improve the world around me. There's always a next step I can take.

One evening Michael and I had one of our rare major disagreements. The cause didn't stick with me, but knowing us, it was likely grammar. We've yet to come to full agreement on which "-ing words" are gerunds or participles, and whether their preceding noun or pronoun should be possessive. I never said life in my house wasn't exciting.

Whatever it was, I likely extracted some larger implication and commentary about my personhood and stormed off into the nearest room with a door that could be definitively closed. But not the bathroom. Far too cliché. There's no elegance in shutting oneself in a bathroom.

So I chose the laundry room.

As I looked around, I realized my mistake. My laundry room is not a place that restores the spirit. While not every home has a dedicated laundry room, every home has some functional equivalent to my laundry room—it might be a corner, a closet, a counter, or a garage. Even if it's not for laundry per se, it's the place where every household task begins and ends. In my laundry room, I have supplies for cleaning, canning, cat and dog caretaking, lightbulb changing, battery replacing, home maintenance, and the all-important utility sink. Plus, because it connects to the garage, it's the thoroughfare for all arrivals and departures, so it amasses recently arrived items, mixed together with ready-to-depart items.

That day the counters were piled high.

Here I was, of my own volition stuck in this place of transition and clutter with my own roiling emotions. The mess before me matched the mess within me. It took me back to another evening with Michael, and another daunting mess all-too-recurring in my house: this time in the kitchen, and the piles were dishes.

He was doing dishes after a long full day, and I was amazed at his ability to tackle that when we were all so very tired. I had done quite a number on the kitchen while cooking, after a day keeping pace with the multi-toddler marathon relay. To me, bringing order out of that heap in the sink felt like unscrambling eggs.

But then Michael spoke two words that again shifted the ground beneath my feet.

"It's finite."

He meant the number of dishes in the sink. They were finite. Countable, quantitative. It shouldn't surprise me that Mr. Spreadsheet would think this way. He finds beauty in data. He gives his spreadsheets whimsical, if cryptic, names like Bigger Boy, PardyLard, Inventory Time Machine. As though they tell a story—which I guess, to him, they do.

His management of numbers is how the soap gets made in pace with the annual double-digit growth. When he came onboard back in 2005, the company did the volume of business in a year that it now does in a week. My husband's whole being functions in a realm where numbers are not squishy and they are not emotional.

I'm less compartmentalized. The physical and emotional realms within me are separated by the finest of lines, and when I'm exhausted or overwhelmed, the line breaks. A pile of laundry has been known to hurt my feelings. A mountain of dishes can bring me to tears.

Michael instead sees the finiteness of the dishes, and I let his point reassure me. One dish done is one less to do. Progress. I realized he was absolutely right. Though most household tasks are finite, I turn them into an emotional battle. The vying of good and evil. Me versus the powers of chaos, with the outcome uncertain. Will I triumph this time?

Michael would shake his head at that drama and get back to washing them piece by piece. And inevitably, the pile diminishes. Order and cleanliness return.

His words became my new mantra to whip out when I'm faced with tasks that threaten to overwhelm. Whether it's folding laundry—

It's finite.

Or doing dishes—

It's finite.

Or picking up the zillions of little bits into which Sadie the Superpup has reduced her latest chew toy—

It's finite.

Or handling the papers that have buried my desk or catching up on unread email. In each instance, one finite item after another, I fend off chaos yet again and have another tangible reminder that I am an active agent in my life.

There's a tension, too, between the finiteness of the immediate task and tasks' cyclical nature. Tomorrow after breakfast, there will be more dishes. There will be more laundry. There will be more chewed toy bits. The trick is to pause in the in-between. To acknowledge and bask in the satisfaction that the task is finished, even if only momentarily. When tomorrow the same task is before me, I'll take it as a reminder that I am still alive and life is flowing on around me.

In this way, Michael and I are both a little right. Mess is finite, but it is also ongoing. On the night of our discord and my flight into the laundry room, I viewed the mess in front of me as a physical manifestation of the chaos I felt within.

And so I started tidying that laundry room. One finite item after another. My pride insisted I make it look like tidying the laundry room was exactly what I had intended on doing with my evening. Item by item. Bagging things to be given away. Carrying them out to the car. Folding, straightening, sorting, tossing. Finite.

Concurrently, the disorder of my mind and heart settled into place, as well.

When I emerged from that room, both the mess and my frustration were gone.

What a blessed gift that we can release our intangible frustrations, sorrows, and confusion through physical effort. We can walk them off, run them off, crochet them off, knead them off, dig them into the garden soil. A clearing, a cleaning, a weeding, a sorting, a de-wrinkling of what is before us and what is within us.

Despite its lackluster appearance, windowless and undecorated, our laundry room is pivotal to the well-being of our house, as are all the out-of-sight closets and cabinets we never show guests. They are the engine rooms, the sources of power that drive the house daily. These spaces are never on public display, but if they're clogged up and bogged down, then there will be problems in the places that are. Stuff will back up elsewhere. Processes will falter.

This is true for the hidden spots in our souls as well. For life to thrive and joy to abound, even the hidden places need order and intention. Our spirits can become as overstuffed with unprocessed thoughts and feelings as any bulging cabinet in our homes. They become dead zones and contaminate more visible areas, shoving agitation and misfiring emotions out into public view. Only focused attention at sorting out each thought and emotion can restore clarity and purpose.

And all-important in this process is reaching out to another. To call the number of the person we may not know well or to reach out to those in our closer circles. To take the risk of saying "help" or "let me help," depending on where we are in our strength phase. To find, more often than not, grace and unexpected wisdom and understanding.

Whether it's the busy little something that soothes the soul or the decluttering of shelves that frees the spirit, the physical and the spiritual intricately dance together. To progress in one realm is to progress in the other. When we're bogged down in one realm, perhaps the way out lies in the other. The laundry room becomes the philosopher's cave.

Now it's time to wash some clothes.

GOING GREEN IN THE LAUNDRY ROOM

As with The Cleaning Cabinet, which may or may not be an actual cabinet in your house, The Laundry Room may not be an actual room and it may not be in your home. Your laundry spot may be in the garage or in a closet off the hall, or out in an apartment's common area, or down the street at the laundromat. Wherever it may be that you launder your clothes and other fabrics, there is a lot that converges in that space.

So many varying activities of life produce laundry, from work to play to sleep to personal care. If you stop to think about it, there's a lot of management involved in taking care of all these fabrics so they can look and perform their best!

RECIPES AND HOW-TOS

MACHINE WASHING LAUNDRY

When I started learning about problematic ingredients in cleaning products, I realized that not only were many of them in laundry detergents, but considering how long fabrics spend touching my body—clothes, sheets, towels (i.e., constantly)—any residues from such ingredients were spending a lot of time on my skin. Conventional laundry detergents intentionally leave residues on fabrics in fabric softeners and lingering fragrance. Instead, I wanted "clean" laundry cleaners, which both the Pure-Castile Soap and the Sal Suds are. There's no need to dilute either one prior to use, even if you're pouring directly onto fabrics. The washing machine will do the diluting for you. If desired, add one of the laundry boosters below.

FOR AN HE WASHING MACHINE WITH A LARGE LOAD, USE ONE OF THE FOLLOWING:

+ 3–4 tablespoons (40–60 ml) Pure-Castile Liquid Soap
+ 1–1½ tablespoons (15–22 ml) Sal Suds
+ 2–2½ tablespoons (30–40 g) Powdered Laundry Soap (recipe below)
+ ¼ cup (60 ml) Soap Cream (page 160)—run with warm or hot water

FOR A STANDARD WASHING MACHINE WITH A LARGE LOAD, USE ONE OF THE FOLLOWING:

+ ⅓–½ cup (80–120 ml) Pure-Castile Liquid Soap
+ 2–3 (30–45 ml) tablespoons Sal Suds
+ ¼–⅓ cup (60–80 g) Powdered Laundry Soap (recipe below)
+ ½ cup (120 ml) Soap Cream (page 160)—run with warm or hot water

WATER TEMPERATURE: Sal Suds and Pure-Castile Liquid Soap work equally well in hot or cold water. For energy saving and clothes longevity, wash on cold. The Powdered Laundry Soap and Soap Cream disperse best in warm or hot water.

POWDERED LAUNDRY SOAP

One 5-ounce bar Pure-Castile Bar Soap
4 cups (920 g) baking soda

Grate soap bar on the fine side of a metal box grater or in a handheld rotary cheese grater. In a food processor, blend grated soap with baking soda, pulsing until evenly blended and granular. Store in an airtight container. Grated soap dissolves best in warm or hot water.

NOTE: When using either the liquid or bar Pure-Castile Soap with hard water, add ½ cup (120 ml) vinegar in HE machines, or 1 cup (240 ml) in standard machines, to the rinse cycle via the fabric softener compartment or a dispensing ball.

Laundry Boosting

These are optional additions for extra cleaning. Choose the least intense methods and the fewest additions in order to prolong the life of the fabrics. Most often, I use Sal Suds alone. If I am using the Pure-Castile Soap, I add the vinegar for fabric softening in hard water. If a load needs extra scrubbing and whitening, I'll add the baking soda.

BAKING SODA

Baking soda, or sodium bicarbonate, the common kitchen leavening agent, is also a gentle way to brighten, whiten, and deodorize laundry. Among three mineral powders commonly used to boost laundry, baking soda is the finest and gentlest. It is a mild alkali with a pH around 8.3.

Add ¼ cup (70 g) per large load in an HE machine, or ½ cup (140 g) in a standard machine, at the beginning of the cycle.

BORAX

With a moderately alkaline pH of 9.5, borax, or sodium borate, is a more intense option for laundry boosting than baking soda. Not only does borax whiten and deodorize fabrics, it softens hard water, thereby boosting the efficacy of the soap or detergent. See discussion of borax safety on page 138.

Add ¼ cup (30 g) per large load in an HE machine, or ½ cup (60 g) in a standard machine, at the beginning of the cycle. Works best in warm or hot water.

WASHING SODA

Washing soda, or sodium carbonate, acts as a water softener and can be helpful when washing laundry with soap, minimizing the interference of the hard water minerals. This is irrelevant if using a detergent like Sal Suds, since the minerals don't interfere there anyway. Washing soda also fights stains and whitens, but with a high pH around 11 to 12, it can be irritating to skin and tissues. Such high alkalinity is not advisable for wool or silk. Washing soda is harsher on clothing than baking soda and can decrease the longevity of clothing.

Add ¼ cup (65 g) per large load in an HE machine, or ½ cup (130 g) in a standard machine, at the beginning of the cycle. Use 1 cup (260 g) for hard water conditions or extra-soiled fabrics. Works best in warm or hot water.

OXYGEN BLEACH

The power behind oxygen bleach is hydrogen peroxide, stabilized into a powder usually as sodium percarbonate. When the powder dissolves in water, the hydrogen peroxide disassociates (separates) and then releases its surplus oxygen. It is this freed oxygen that fights stains, breaking the chemical bonds of chromophores, the components of stains that give them their color. While oxygen bleach is a much safer option than chlorine bleaches (see discussion of chlorine bleach safety on page 139), you should understand its limitations: soap or detergent accelerates the oxygen release, which reduces oxygen bleach's stain fighting opportunity. This is why it is best to use oxygen bleach as a presoak rather than in the washing cycle. Once oxygen bleach has doffed its hydrogen peroxide, it becomes simply sodium carbonate (i.e., washing soda—see discussion above). It is always best to use the fewest products needed to achieve the desired results. Use oxygen bleach when less intensive methods of laundering have not succeeded.

Use as a presoak ahead of laundering with the Pure-Castile Soap or Sal Suds. Works best in warm or hot water.

HAND-WASHING DELICATES

Hand-washing clothes certainly extends their life. Machine washing is much rougher on fabrics, especially when buttons or zippers are involved. More and more, I find myself hand-washing clothes. It is so easy to toss a blouse or dress in the bathroom sink while I take my morning shower. By the time I'm dressed the blouse is ready for its final steps, and it dries while I'm out for the day. This does not take a tremendous amount of time.

1 capful (about 1 tablespoon or 15 ml) Pure-Castile Soap OR
½ capful (½ tablespoon or 7.5 ml) Sal Suds
1 gallon (4 L) cold water

1. Combine the cleaner and water in a sink or basin. Submerge the garment and swish thoroughly, gently squeezing the water through the fabric. Let soak for 10 minutes. Swish again to release loosened grime, focusing on soiled spots. Drain and refill the sink with clean water to rinse.

2. To condition natural fibers like silk and wool, after washing and rinsing fabric, add 1 cup (240 ml) white vinegar to cold water. Swish garment and rinse once more with clean water.

3. With a towel, gently press excess water out of fabric. Do not wring. Lay stretchy fabrics flat to dry and hang sturdy and lightweight fabrics.

WASHING BEDDING

Although I usually do my laundry on cold to extend the life of my fabrics, for bedding I kick up the heat to high since heat helps loosen oils and kills dust mites.[43]

FOR HE WASHING MACHINE:

3 tablespoons–¼ cup (45–60 ml) Pure-Castile Liquid Soap OR
1 1½ tablespoons (15–22.5 ml) Sal Suds

FOR A STANDARD WASHING MACHINE:

⅓–½ cup (80–120 ml) Pure-Castile Liquid Soap OR

2–3 tablespoons (30–45 m) Sal Suds

HOW TO:

1. When using Pure-Castile Soap with hard water, add ½ cup (120 ml) in HE machines, or 1 cup (240 ml) vinegar in standard machines, to the rinse cycle via the fabric softener compartment or a dispensing ball.

2. Set the washer at the hottest setting. Dry the bedding on the hottest setting.

3. Because sheets keep other bedding away from our bodies, blankets and comforters don't need to be washed as often. However, they still can accumulate dust, so monthly trips through the "air fluff" cycle of a dryer and a minimum of twice-a-year full washing is still a good idea. Be sure your machine is large enough to handle your bulky bedding. If a machine is too small, not only will the cleansers and the rinse water not be able to circulate fully in the washer, but in the dryer, certain parts could get excessively hot, even to the point of burning, while others still remain damp. You might need to head to your nearest laundromat with an industrial-sized machine.

Frequency of Washing Bedding

Just as important as the question of "how" to wash bedding is "how often." If you think about the number of hours you spend in your bed each week—if you follow the recommended 7 to 9 hours a night, that's 49 to 56 hours a week. Imagine wearing clothes for over two days straight. They would need a wash, just as your sheets do weekly. Perhaps if you shower before bed, sleep in long pajamas, and aren't generally a hot sleeper, you can get away with every two weeks. If you share your bed with any canines, felines, or other such friends, weekly sheet washing is a must.

Sheets and pillowcases, with their direct and lengthy skin contact, accumulate a significant buildup of sweat, oils, and dust. Then you have the microscopic critters who feed on all that: bacteria and dust mites. (Yes, ew!) All this needs to be removed regularly. Dust mites in particular are a common allergen.

You'll see in my washing recommendations that hot water and high-heat drying are best for eliminating dust mites. But this combo of high heat and frequent washings can take a toll on fabrics, so for fabric longevity, start with high-quality 100 percent cotton fabrics with a moderately high thread count (300-plus). You may pay a little more up front, but over time, buying quality saves money and makes better use of environmental resources. As my mom says, "When you buy quality, you only cry once."

Washing Down and Down Alternatives

If your down- and alternative down-filled gear—like comforters, blankets, pillows, sleeping bags, or jackets—aren't as warm or as fluffy as they once were, it is possible that the fill is weighed down by grime and needs a wash. Given that washing and drying is a pummeling process that can wear down the items, reserve washing until necessary. Air out gear after each use and spot-clean items promptly. For brevity, I refer to "down" here to include either down or down alternative, which have the same washing instructions.

Down is one of those odd luxury items that might be better off washed by machine than by hand. Also, unless the care instructions say otherwise, don't dry-clean your down.

Follow the Care Label

Manufacturers know their products best. Follow the instructions listed on the care label. If you're like me and you remove labels, tape or staple them in a little notebook by your washer.

If the care instructions say to use a "mild detergent," then Sal Suds fits the bill. This is a rare instance in which the Pure-Castile Soap is not interchangeable with the Sal Suds. If there is any hardness in the water, the

Pure-Castile Soap will react and potentially leave a residue on the fill. My usual recommendation for a follow-up vinegar rinse may too acidic for the longevity of the down or down alternative. So stick with the Sal Suds.

Wash down-filled items by themselves. Do not toss them in with your regular laundry. They wash and especially dry at far different rates than your average laundry.

SPOT-CLEANING DOWN

If all your item needs is a little cleanup around the edges or a smudge here and there, try spot-cleaning first.

1 tablespoon (15 ml) Sal Suds in 1 cup (240 ml) water

1. Dip a clean washcloth into this solution, wringing out the excess, and rub the spots and smudges. Refrain from saturating the internal down.

2. Then dip a new washcloth into clean water to rinse the areas, again taking care not to soak the item.

3. Let air dry thoroughly. If you think you may have saturated the internal down, proceed with the drying section below.

NOTE: This method is preferable to spraying the spots, which may cause more moisture to penetrate into the down.

MACHINE WASHING DOWN

If spot-cleaning is insufficient and the care label permits, proceed with a complete washing.

+ Check for tears in the casing and repair if needed. (Pause for a moment and envision the featherstorm a small rip would create in your dryer.)
+ For jackets, vests, or sleeping bags, zip zippers and loosen elastic cords. Empty pockets. Turn inside out.

✦ Use a machine with no agitator, which can rip the thin casings on down items. A front-loader or top-loading HE machine with no agitator would be best.

✦ Use a machine large enough to allow for water flow around the item. Home washers are probably not big enough to wash a sleeping bag. You'll need to head to a commercial laundromat. (If the machine may have been used previously with a strong detergent, run an empty rinse cycle through it first.)

FOR AN HE MACHINE
½ tablespoon (7.5 ml) Sal Suds

FOR A REGULAR WASHER (WITHOUT AN AGITATOR)
1 tablespoon (15 ml) Sal Suds (about half the normal amount for laundry)

1. Set the machine for warm (85°F/30°C) on a delicate cycle with an extra rinse cycle.

2. If your washer does not have a soap dispenser, start the waterflow and disperse the Sal Suds in the water. (Do not pour the Sal Suds onto the dry down-filled item; this could create very sudsy spots that are difficult to rinse.)

3. Once the wash cycle and the extra rinse cycle are done, inspect the item to see if all the soap is rinsed out. Rub your hand over the fabric and check for suds. Squeeze the fabric and see if it sounds soapy.

Do not use fabric softeners, which leave residues on fabrics and would weigh on down.

Can You Hand-Wash Down?

Yes, if it's a small item, you can hand-wash. However, in a match between me and a water-logged king-sized comforter, I know my comforter would win. But a jacket or personal blanket? You could probably wash those by hand adequately in a sink or bathtub. The key is having enough room for water flow and agitation around the item and providing enough agitation and rinsing action to draw out the grime.

DRYING DOWN

Sufficiently drying a down-filled item is critical to successful cleaning. If not dried well and thoroughly, your down will be clumpy, ineffective, and likely to mildew.

Down and down alternative can take a long time to dry. Expect up to 2 to 3 hours in a dryer for a heavy, high loft jacket. Much longer for a sleeping bag or comforter. Drying in a dryer is more reliable than air drying because the motion brings more airflow around all sides of the feathers or fibers, lifting and separating them, thereby increasing dryness.

If you're using the washer to wash, run the spin cycle a few extra times to get as much water out of the item as possible. There's nothing like good old centrifugal force to throw the water out.

1. Put the item in the dryer with no other laundry.

2. Toss in 2 to 3 clean tennis balls or dryer balls. These are key to keeping the down in motion and breaking up clumps.

3. Do not use dryer sheets, which deposit residues on fabrics.

4. Set the dryer to low heat for a long cycle. You'll probably need several cycles for larger items.

5. Take the item out of the dryer every 20 to 30 minutes to fluff and reposition.

6. The item is done when it feels dry to the touch, is light for its size, and fluffs well with no clumping.

Don't take shortcuts. Don't turn up the heat. Not only do burnt feathers smell awful, but the drying time is all about the amount of airflow, and heat doesn't add to this.

How to Store Down or Down Alternative

Store these items uncompressed and in a dry spot. Compression can break the feathers and compress the insulation fibers, reducing the loft and thus the warmth. This means down comforters should not be stored over summer in vacuum bags. Sleeping bags should not be stored in their sacks but should hang free or be loosely gathered in a stuffsack.

WASHING CLOTH DIAPERS
AND MENSTRUAL PADS

This is another of the few scenarios in which I specifically recommend Sal Suds over Pure-Castile Soap. If the washing water contains any hardness, the soap could react with minerals and leave a film on diapers or menstrual pads that would make them less absorbent. Sal Suds is immune to hard water, while still free from synthetic fragrance, dye, fabric softeners, bleach, or enzymes that might reduce absorbency or leave residues that could harm sensitive skin.

Because of the great variety in product types, refer to your manufacturer's recommendations for pretreatment, soaking, washing temperature, and drying method. Dispose of any loose material before washing.

IN AN HE MACHINE:

1 tablespoon (15 ml) Sal Suds

IN A STANDARD MACHINE:

2 tablespoons (30 ml) Sal Suds

OPTIONAL ADD-INS:

2 tablespoons (25 g) baking soda in an HE machine, or ¼ cup (50 g) in a standard machine, for extra whitening, brightening, and deodorizing

¼ cup (60 ml) distilled white vinegar in an HE machine, or ½ cup (120 ml) in a standard machine, for extra deodorizing, especially of the ammonia smell

1. Wash per manufacturer's recommendations with cold or hot water.

2. Air drying in sunshine is a great way to add some extra whitening to the diapers or pads while using free energy. Do not use fabric softeners with diapers or pads.

Stain Treatments and Pretreatments

Treat stains as soon as possible. Rinse stain with cold water to remove as much soil as possible before applying stain treatment. Hot water can set many types of stains. Even if you do not have any of the following cleaners handy, get the garment soaking in water, the universal solvent.

Spray with Sal Suds at a 1:1 Dilution

I use this more than anything else. It's a quick way to cover a swath of fabric from ring around the collar to underarm stains. I keep one bottle in my closet for quick action when I notice a stain, as well as one in my laundry room. Even if I won't be washing the item until the next day, I still apply these treatments as soon as possible. With delicate fabrics or dyes, please do a spot test first.

Apply Undiluted Sal Suds or Pure-Castile Liquid Soap

For deeper stains, use one of these straight out of the bottle. Sal Suds has a step up on the Pure-Castile Soap for stain fighting, but both work well. Since so little Sal Suds is needed for general laundry, make sure you deduct the amount you apply directly onto stains from the overall amount needed for a load.

Soak

For super set stains, apply pretreatment, and then soak the fabric in water for 30 to 60 minutes before adding it to the wash cycle. Check the stain before putting the garment in the dryer, which would set residual stains. If the stain remains, reapply the stain treatment, soak, and wash again.

Tips for Energy Efficiency and Fabric Longevity

Advancements in the technology of our cleaning solutions and machines have paved the way for much greater energy efficiency and reduced wear and tear on our clothes. Top load washers that carry an Energy Star label use 25 percent less energy and about 70 to 75 percent less water than washers 20 years ago.[44]

However, the biggest hurdle to realizing these benefits is consumer behavior.[45] In fact, overall energy and water use for laundry is up despite these technological advancements. We own more clothing and wash it more often while using water that's too hot and too much cleaning solution.

Doing any of the following will help increase the sustainability of your laundry practices and the longevity of your clothes.

+ Only wash clothes when they need it.
+ Air out clothes after wearing to extend time between launderings.
+ Hang or fold clothes promptly.
+ Spot-clean to postpone laundering.
+ Hand-wash clothes, especially delicates.
+ Treat stains promptly.
+ Wash full loads.
+ Use cold water for most loads (machines and cleaners are designed for it).
+ Use hot water strategically to combat sickness or clean particularly grimy rags or to eradicate dust mites and other microscopic life.
+ Use the fewest and least intense laundry boosters as needed to get fabrics clean.
+ Use less soap or detergent for smaller or less soiled loads.
+ Use the maximum spin cycle in the washer to extract water and reduce dry time.
+ Avoid fabric softeners and dryer sheets, which coat and degrade fabrics.
+ Dry loads promptly before mildew can form and necessitate rewashing.
+ Minimize dryer use. Air dry clothes.
+ Use sunlight to dry and bleach laundry.
+ Use wool dryer balls in the dryer to shorten dry time and reduce static.

+ Clean the lint trap after every load.
+ Clear your dryer vent regularly—the one that vents outside.
+ Buy quality. Buy less.
+ Store clothes well.
+ Keep the humidity low in closets and drawers with moisture absorbers.
+ Use cedar planks, balls, or hangers if moths are prevalent.
+ Fold heavy or stretchy items like sweaters so they don't stretch out on hangers.
+ Invest in quality hangers, like wood or velvet, that maintain your clothes' shape.
+ Learn basic mending so that a missing button or open seam doesn't mean the end.

BONUS TIPS FOR CLOTHING SUSTAINABILITY

The clothing industry is incredibly opaque, and it is difficult to ensure that clothing lines are fully ethical and sustainable. However, keeping clothes in use longer helps reduce clothing waste.

+ Buy at resale shops, consignment sales, and thrift stores—or their online counterparts.
+ When you're tired of clothing that still has a lot of life in it, host a clothing swap with friends, sell at consignment, hold a yard sale, or donate items.
+ With children's clothes that are outgrown before they're outworn, bless a friend with kids by handing them down.

The Problem with Fabric Softeners and Dryer Sheets

Fabric softener and dryer sheets can be hard to pry out of the grip of even the most deeply green people. For many they are the smell of clean laundry. Discuss fabric softener and dryer sheets together because they are the same thing. Dryer sheets are squares coated in fabric softener.

But what is fabric softener?

Fabric softener is lubricant for fabrics, which I realize doesn't sound very attractive. What happened to the snuggly bears and bursting flowers?

Fabric softener works by depositing a thin film, usually made from a silicone or cationic quaternary ammonium compound, aka "quats." This coating increases lubricity so that your hand slides smoothly over the fabrics and the fabrics slide smoothly against each other. It's the same technology that is used in hair conditioner—sometimes even the same ingredient. This lubricant on fabrics reduces static electricity and wrinkles.

So, with all this talk of softening clothes, reducing static, and smoothing wrinkles, I'm not doing a great job of convincing you of the ills of fabric softeners. Here's the downside.

These lubricant residues build up on fabric in wash after wash, creating a layer of dinginess. This buildup also degrades the fabrics and decreases the life span of the item.

Certain fabrics should never be laundered with softeners because the residues interfere with the function of the fabric. Moisture-wicking fabrics used for athletic wear lose their ability to absorb moisture from the body. Similarly, cloth diapers and towels become less absorbent. In these scenarios, fabric softener nullifies the fabrics' basic function.

And then we get to the problem of fragrance. As I've mentioned several times already, many problematic chemicals lie within the realm of fragrance and its 3,000 potential ingredients. Fragrances in laundry products are strong. I can tell on my morning walk which houses are doing laundry, and I live in the country, with acres between the houses.

I completely understand the associations of the smell of laundry and clean. It is a major part of how laundry products are sold because marketers know the power of scent. People may say they want their fabrics to look bright and white, but often the first thing they do when a load is done washing is hold it up to their nose and smell it.

If these scents are designed to cling to fabrics for several cycles of the moon, imagine how long they will cling to the inside of your lungs? Fragrances are meant to stay, and they have no cognition to decide whether they stay on the fabrics or in your lungs.

Immediate maladies such as respiratory ailments and migraines linked to laundry fragrance have a large body of evidence. One 2016 study found that over 12.5 percent of respondents reported irritation from scented laundry products that were vented outside.[46] Another study of fabric softeners found emissions caused lung irritation and limited airflow.[47]

Concerns with laundry are further intensified because, unlike other surfaces in our house that we casually touch, we are in constant full-body contact with the fabrics we launder. We wear them, we dry with them, we sleep on them. Any problematic residues that are on the fabrics and any fumes released by them have every opportunity to bother our skin and enter our bodies. With the use of fabric softeners, residues are guaranteed by design. This guarantees direct skin contact. Studies show that nearly 1 in 10 people exhibit signs of allergic contact dermatitis from fragrance when tested in a controlled patch testing.[48]

The downsides of fabric softeners go beyond impacts to our health and fabrics. One study out of Japan identified fabric softeners and laundry detergents as the most toxic of household detergents that could end up in waterways.[49] Fabric softeners do not break down in water, which makes them particularly problematic for septic systems, where they can form a waxy layer on the surfaces of tanks. Further, the quaternary compounds in fabric softeners have disinfectant properties, and at volume can disrupt the needed bacterial action septic systems use to operate. Septic service companies regularly advise against using fabric softeners.[50]

Can you circumvent this concern of fabric softeners by using dryer sheets instead? Dryer sheets serve the same function as liquid fabric softeners—coating fabrics with lubricants and artificial scents—and leave the same problematic residues behind to irritate skin and lungs. As far as environmental impact, you are exchanging one problem for another. Dryer sheets have an afterlife issue. They are a single-use item, conventionally made out of nonwoven polyester that does not break down. There have been advances in green technology, creating sheets made from compostable materials, but anything that is short-term or single use is an incredible waste of resources and something we need to move away from.

Alternatives to Fabric Softeners and Dryer Sheets

For Softening and Static Reduction
+ Use vinegar in place of liquid fabric softener or spray a clean washcloth lightly with vinegar and toss in the dryer.
+ Use wool dryer balls for softening, static reduction, and reducing drying time.
+ Air dry clothes to reduce static caused by friction of fabrics rubbing together.

For De-Wrinkling
+ Remove clothes from dryer immediately at the end of the cycle and fold or hang.
+ Wet your dryer balls and throw them in with the wrinkled clothes; check after 20 minutes.
+ Air dry clothes.

For Scenting
+ Use well-sealed herbal sachets in the dryer. Lavender, mint, and lemon balm are great options.
+ Store clothes with herbal sachets.
+ Store clothes with a cotton pad sprinkled with a few drops of essential oil. Be sure the essential oil does not touch clothes to smudge them.
+ Accustom yourself to less scent in your fabrics.

Ask Lisa

Q Can I use essential oils in my dryer, such as on my wool dryer balls?

A This is not a good idea for a reason called flash point. Flash point is the temperature at which a vaporized oil will catch fire if an ignition source is present. Many common essential oils, such as all citrus, fir, spruce, bergamot, and nutmeg, have very low flash points, lower than even the delicate heat setting on an average dryer. New, well-maintained dryers have a heat range usually between 125°F–135°F (52°C–57°C), but lint buildup or age can cause them to run hotter. A ready ignition source is static. Just one static spark has the potential to ignite these low oils. Take sweet orange oil—my favorite scent— but with a flash point of 115°F (46°C), it's a terrible idea in the dryer. Plus, oils run the risk of smudging clean clothes.

Instead: See the sachet options on page 136.

Q Does regular laundering get rid of any germs in my laundry?

A Yes. Soap or detergent used in the wash cycle removes germs effectively, even in cold water. For especially grimy loads or in times of sickness, you can boost the heat if the fabrics will tolerate it, but regularly washing laundry on hot is unnecessary and a waste of resources.

Q What's wrong with dry-cleaning?

A Dry-cleaning is an incredibly misleading word. Dry-cleaning is not dry. It's just waterless. I had long envisioned that dry-cleaning involved some intense application of powders that magically lifted stains. Instead, the process uses petroleum-based solvents.

In the early days of dry-cleaning, kerosene was the solvent of choice. Combustion risk was high. Then, for about a century, perchloroethylene, or perc for short, was the norm, but studies finding it to be a toxic air contami-

continues

nant and an anticipated human carcinogen have led the EPA to ban its use in areas where people also live, and have given it more stringent standards in general. California has banned its use altogether beginning January 1, 2023.[51]

There are several alternatives to perc, such as liquid carbon dioxide or even certain water cleaning techniques. However, there are pros and cons to all of these alternatives, including other health and safety hazards, effectiveness, and cost.[52] If you can't avoid a "dry-clean only" garment, look for dry-cleaners that use alternatives to perc and be sure to air out dry-cleaned clothing once home.

Q **The washing instructions say to use a mild detergent. How do I know if my detergent is mild?**

A A mild detergent is a simple cleaner with a moderate pH and no enzymes, abrasives, or residues. Look for a simple, short ingredient list. Any enzymes would either end in "-ase" or be trademarked with an ®. Any abrasives would be evident by a gritty feel to the detergent. Residues would come from fabric softening agents—look for dimethicone or siloxanes—or from lingering fragrances. Enzymes and abrasives have benefits in other cleaning situations, but are more aggressive and should not be used where mild is required. Both Dr. Bronner's Pure-Castile Soap and Sal Suds qualify as mild.

Q **Is borax safe? What about washing soda?**

A Borax, aka sodium borate or the salt of boric acid, has sparked fierce debate among green circles as to its safety and whether it belongs among the ranks of green cleaners. Both sides debate ardently and with the best of intentions.

With a moderately alkaline pH of 9.5, borax has myriad industrial uses in glass and ceramics, soaps and detergents, cosmetics, preservatives, solvents, pesticides, fertilizers, and fire retardants. In households it is marketed as a laundry booster and all-purpose cleaner.

The "No, it's not green" contingent points out that borax dust can cause respiratory and eye irritation, even damaging corneas. It readily absorbs through damaged skin, as well as through mucous membranes as in the mouth, nose, throat, and eyes. Those with preexisting skin conditions, such as eczema, are more susceptible to irritation from borax. Swallowing small to moderate amounts can cause various gastrointestinal upsets, and large amounts require medical attention and can even lead to death.

Those in the "Yes, it's green" camp tout that it is a renewable resource that naturally recurs in the residue of dry seasonal lake beds, and it is biodegradable. Borax does not irritate or absorb through healthy skin.[53] It is not volatile. The most highly exposed occupations (e.g., borax miners) exhibit no evidence of harm, and the large amounts required for ingestion harm are unrealistic.[54]

And herein lies the concern with borax. Properly used, it is effective and harmless, with no problematic residues for people or planet. Even some deviation from normal use leads to no lasting harm. But too much for too long, ingested at volume or misapplied in the extreme can cause serious harm.

All in all, while borax is not the most villainous ingredient, there are usually milder options for the job. Personally, I start with baking soda, which is even milder, and only boost more when needed.

While borax has been the focus of the debates, nearly everything I've said about it holds true for washing soda if misused, except more extreme. I don't know why the attention has been more on borax. Washing soda's pH, at 11 to 12 compared to borax's 9.5. At this level of alkalinity, washing soda is slightly corrosive and irritating to the skin. It will also darken aluminum. It is an effective water softening agent and fights stains, but it should only be used when truly needed, and always handled with care.

Q **What's wrong with chlorine bleach in the laundry? It seems safer since I'm not directly handling it.**

A Because of the agitation of the machine plus the heat of the water, what we put in the washing machine still becomes airborne. There are still problematic fumes that hit our lungs. If something is antimicrobial—strongly so with bleach—it is not merely anti-*bad*-microbial. It does not follow a targeted instruction to eliminate only a specific microbe and then, once it accomplishes its mission, go quietly away. Antimicrobials wipe out wide swaths of microbes. Most washing machines empty into two systems: the septic or the sewer. I happen to have a septic system, which is wholly dependent on bacteria and enzymes to work. Killing them would shut down the system.[55]

Finally, chlorine bleach is a strong corrosive material and can oxidize metal, impacting the longevity of a machine.[56] Beyond the laundry room, it can dull shiny finishes on sinks, bathtubs, and other porcelain enamel faces. Bleach will also darken aluminum and make linoleum brittle.[57]

Two final things I want to encourage you to keep in mind about chlorine bleach. First, green ingredients can't make non-green ingredients green. Using bleach with Pure-Castile Soap and vinegar does not make bleach safer. Second, remember the risk/benefit balance in cleaning. Make sure the benefit gained is worth the risk. Regular use of bleach is overkill, in every sense of the word, and there are good alternatives as mentioned above.

CHAPTER 4
THE KITCHEN

*You will teach them to fly, but they will not fly your flight. You will
teach them to dream, but they will not dream your dream. You will
teach them to live, but they will not live your life. Nevertheless,
in every flight, in every life, in every dream, the print of the way
you taught them will remain.*
—**MOTHER TERESA**

And there went another blender.

About the only thing that miffed my mom about my dad's creative genius was how many of her kitchen implements ended up in the garage in his impromptu home laboratory. No idea could wait until the next day, when he'd be at work with its fully stocked lab. He needed to act before the inspiration faded. And so blenders, knives, whisks of all sorts disappeared from the kitchen.

My dad, whom we called Pop, was a great chemist, a great inventor, and a great cook. He held several patents on formulations himself and created many more on behalf of employers. Class A foams for firefighting, gelled fuels for controlled burns (my Mom did put her foot down on home tests of those), industrial floor waxes and lubricants, an artificial snow called Snofoam for movies. He contrived devices to use them as well.

When he went into private consulting and all his work centered at our house, it wasn't unusual for our corner to attract a crowd of curious onlookers. I'd come home from school to what looked like a freak snow-storm blanketing our suburban L.A. home. He'd been testing Snofoam, which not only looks fantastically snowy, but is a ton of fun to play in. Or perhaps the house would be surrounded by seven firetrucks, but my first thought was always that he must be doing a demonstration, not that the house was ablaze.

His segue to cooking isn't surprising. Cooking, after all, is edible chemistry. His cooking was marvelous. Instinctive. Innovative. Whim-sical. Delicious. Except for that last, all the same could be said about his chemistry.

I learned the pizzazz of cooking from my dad. We were glad he didn't cook often because he used every pan in the kitchen and it fell on the rest of us to clean it up. He could never re-create exactly what he cooked, which taught us to appreciate the moment. The next time would be magnificent, but it would never be the same.

His barbecue sauce was a case in point. Always delectable, but if writ-ten, his recipe would say, "Open the fridge and use what's there." Mus-tards, syrups, salad dressings. I tried several times to watch him closely to capture it, but the only consistent ingredient was my mom's homemade plum jam. Funny—I don't remember the taste of my mom's homemade plum jam. I guess because it always ended up in the barbecue sauce.

My dad's cooking was outlandish. Prime rib slow roasted in front of the fireplace suspended by rope and turnbuckle from the ceiling. Quite the sight in our suburban Los Angeles home. I have no idea how he kept the dog away. His "fast foods" were peach crêpes and omelets.

As my dad in his cooking was extravagant, bordering on the outra-geous, my mom was consistent and comforting. The epitome of the well-balanced plate: one protein, one starch, two veggies. Her meals nourished us every day without giving us a tornado to clean up after. Littering my own recipe books are Mom's Spaghetti, Mom's Chili, Mom's Stroganoff, Mom's Macaroni and Cheese. And always a gorgeous green salad.

It is the ultimate of luxuries that I grew up with both these styles in my house. They both live within me now—the everyday consistency and the occasional flair. The comfort of routine and the pop of celebration.

This is why the kitchen is my solace and therapy for so much of life. I lean into the steady routine of my mom's example when days are frenzied, making the reliable, known foods. But then on days where I crave an outlet for joy, you'll find me there, channeling my dad, making something lavish and unnecessary.

There wasn't much of a boundary with my dad between his chemistry and his cooking. I remember how he once judged the caliber of a new brand of bar soap on the market by nibbling a corner. "Too alkaline," he pronounced. "It'll be off the market in a year." And it was.

My dad was self-taught. He barely graduated high school, only buckling down after realizing in the spring of his senior year that he was on the brink of failing the required math. He eked out with a D. Funny that he married a math teacher.

My dad joined the Navy after high school, which he credits with giving his life direction and discipline. He rose from the bottom rung as a Seaman Recruit to Chief Petty Officer, the highest enlisted Naval rank. After the Navy, his professional life followed a similar course. He began at a chemical manufacturing company as "chief bottle washer," in my mom's words, and rose to be the company's vice president, before leaving to found his own chemical consulting company. He continued to run this even after he assumed the presidency of Dr. Bronner's upon his father's decline. His path should give late bloomers everywhere hope.

If you met my mom, she would strike you as kind, reserved, intelligent, put-together, trustworthy, and steady. While she does a great deal of very important work, both as CFO of Dr. Bronner's and in numerous civic organizations, as well as her church, she is never frenzied. She plans her time well and allows for contingencies. She's ordered. Calm. Intentional.

She and my dad were perfect foils, and they so appreciated and enjoyed each other's strengths. My dad's exuberance partnered with my mom's steadiness. My dad's dreaming partnered with my mom's planning.

However, lest I leave you with the impression that my dad had the market cornered when it came to pushing boundaries, let me tell you how my parents met.

As my dad would tell it, they met at a social (I think that means "party") when he refused to pass my mom, a smoker in her youth, the ashtray she requested. She then threatened to use his palm. My dad was smitten and asked her to dance. I asked my mom for her side of the story, and she doesn't have an alternate version of that event.

My dad said that later, when he was driving her to another social (Goodness!), she reached her foot over from the passenger side and hit the accelerator, saying, "Can't this thing go any faster?"

My mom doesn't have an alternate version of that incident either.

I share this not to blow her cover but to alert you that when you encounter the composed, profoundly competent person that she is, know that still waters run deep and there is a good bit of waggishness beneath the surface.

This trait has surfaced over the years, markedly one night several decades later, when she was over at my house for dinner. I was pouring frozen peas into a pan to cook and looked down to find my three-year-old daughter smacking her lips at my hip, all prepared with a plastic cup, in hopeful anticipation of getting some peas. She's always liked peas.

"You can't eat the peas yet," I told her. "I need to cook them."

"Why can't she?" asked my mom.

My world tilted, as did my mental dinner plate with its one protein-one starch-two veggies. The peas were rolling off the edge, and this was the person who had taught me that arrangement.

I could think of no reason she couldn't eat the peas frozen other than that I never had.

"Do you want to eat the peas frozen?" I asked her.

Vigorous nodding.

And so was birthed a dinnertime revolution. We started having appetizers. Sounds fancy, but they really were just the vegetables I'd planned for dinner, ahead of time. If a kid eats vegetables as an appetizer—frozen or otherwise—the kid is eating vegetables. Eaten as an appetizer means they are seasoned with the most irresistible spice of all: hunger. Plus, it buys me time to make the rest of dinner.

My mom's example of having structures but knowing when to break them has taught me much. In my work, I can see traces of both my parents.

My dad learned by doing and was endlessly curious. A "let's see what happens" approach. I recall one day helping him with some experiment, and I mismeasured an ingredient. Instead of scolding, he told me that many discoveries were made because of mistakes, and so we continued. When I mismeasured another ingredient, though, he explained that there now were too many variables and we'd need to start over.

Instead of my garage, the kitchen is my lab, where I both cook and test my GIY concoctions, sometimes disconcertingly at the same time. My family knows not to assume the edibility of anything bubbling on the stove or stored in mason jars. I'm notoriously bad at labeling things. It could be marshmallow cream or deodorant, Jell-O or soap jellies, whipped cream or soap cream. What looks like a platter of fondant-wrapped cakes might be a batch of beeswax and lint fire starters. (Sorry, Michael.) What looks like grated cheese in a jar could be grated bar soap. (Not sure I'm sorry about that one, kids. It was pretty funny.)

So much life and memory revolves around the kitchen and the kitchen table, both in my childhood and in my parenthood. Regularly gathering with my family around the dinner table has been the single most important parenting act in my day.

It's where my children have learned to sit and be patient and listen and that good things are coming. Where they've learned social graces and what to do when you don't like something. It's where the kids have heard that sometimes adults have hard days, and where the adults have heard that sometimes kids have hard days, too.

Our table is a sacred place. Not because it's fancy—it's sturdy wood with some knicks—but because a regular unification happens there. For years, five individual lives regularly merged back into one family, night after night.

For this reason, we light a candle when we eat together. We celebrate the immediate victory of getting everyone, and the food, to the table. No small feat some days. We recognize the luxury of being able to gather in peace, comfort, and abundance. These recent days, we cherish the time together, becoming rarer as the kids have begun to launch into their own adult lives. Having all of us at the table is a novelty.

At the table, the physical nourishing of our bodies becomes the unifying and strengthening, our spirits. With a candle flame, the physical transitions to the ethereal.

GOING GREEN IN THE KITCHEN

Back in The Cleaning Cabinet I shared how to make many of the solutions that I use for cleaning the kitchen. A bottle of the GIY All-Purpose Cleaning Spray and the Scouring Powder live under my kitchen sink for cleaning counters, stovetops, sinks. A foaming pump dispenser (from The Bath and Bedroom) sits beside the sink for hands and even individual dishes or pieces of fruit. However, the kitchen certainly has some unique considerations, which I'll go over below.

Although we are in the kitchen, we are not going to veer into cooking. But I do have a few "recipes" for the house that are easiest to do in the kitchen. Be sure you do a better job labeling what's what than I do.

Three Paths to Clean: Mechanical, Thermal, Chemical

Before we continue, I want to pause here to consider the three primary pathways to getting something clean. They all factor into how we care for our kitchens but have impacts throughout the house. Michael introduced this idea to me, and it has really helped me think through how I clean and, more importantly, the intensity of my cleaners.

MECHANICAL CLEANING: Physically removing dirt and debris. Think of a broom, which is a large example, that pushes dirt off a surface. Also, vacuuming, scouring, scrubbing, scraping, wiping, or dusting with a damp cloth. I start with this pathway because I daresay it is the most essential pathway to getting things clean. Loose dirt and debris must first be removed from surfaces in order for the other cleaning pathways to be effective. If, for whatever reason, all you are able to do is mechanically clean, this will go a long way toward keeping your space hygienic and attractive. Regular dusting and vacuuming removes the largest mass of contaminants from the house: hair and dander from animals and people, decomposing insects and their emissions, food debris, lint and fibers, soil, soot, settled particles from cooking, and many different hazardous chemicals. Household dust regularly contains PFAS (the "forever chemicals" discussed on page 238), lead, arsenic, and even DDT.

THERMAL CLEANING: Heat or cold. Heat agitates molecules, causing grease to loosen from surfaces and speeding up reactions, which can make chemical cleaners more effective. Hot laundry cycles are effective against dust mites, as is cold: put soft textiles like comforters and pillows in a chest freezer for a day or two. A self-cleaning oven uses extreme heat to blast away deposits. Steam mops use heat to loosen floor gunk. A few cautions about heat, though: sometimes heat can worsen stains, as in the case of blood or chocolate, where heat causes the stain to set. Also, while extremely high heat can kill bacteria, this is not relevant to cleaning our hands or bodies, or

continues

to anything we clean with our hands. The level of heat required to kill bacteria would severely burn our skin, and soap is enough to clean these surfaces.

CHEMICAL CLEANING: Cleaning at the molecular level. While I know the connotations around the word "chemical" can be negative, I need you to hold on to the bigger definition: chemistry is the interaction between atoms or molecules. In this regard, as far as cleaning goes, castile soap is a chemical. Vinegar (acetic acid) is a chemical. Bleach and ammonia are also chemicals, so chemicals are a vast realm. As far as cleaning goes, chemicals work at the molecular level, such as with micelle formation, in the case of surfactants, which use the charges of the molecules, or by forming or breaking bonds with contaminants or pathogens. This can be a mild interaction, again in the case of soap, with few side effects, or a very powerful reaction with extensive repercussions, as is the case with bleach. While chemicals are an important tool in cleaning, use them strategically and wisely.

IN COMBINATION: Often, we use more than one of the cleaning pathways at the same time. When hand-washing dishes, we start with some detergent (chemical), add hot water (thermal), and scrub with a brush (mechanical). In our washing machines, we might set the water to hot (thermal), add some detergent (chemical), and let the machine agitate the clothes clean (mechanical). Even for ourselves, we step into a hot shower (thermal), apply some soap (chemical), and scrub ourselves down (mechanical). These combinations mean we do not need to use as intensive cleaners as we would if we were using just one alone.

How Soap Is Made

I find the soapmaking reaction beautiful. It's so efficiently tidy with no waste and produces something eminently useful. It's fitting to discuss this in the kitchen, where many good things are made, even though we're not going to eat this one.

Soap is made of two things: oil or fat and a strong alkali. That's it. Other compounds may be added for fun, but at its core, soap is only oil and alkali. The oil or fat can be plant-based, like Dr. Bronner's coconut/olive/palm kernel/hempseed/jojoba blend, or it can be animal-based, such as tallow (beef) or lanolin (sheep). The alkali needs to be something strong enough to break apart the oil/fat molecules. Sodium hydroxide is used to make solid bar soap, and potassium hydroxide is

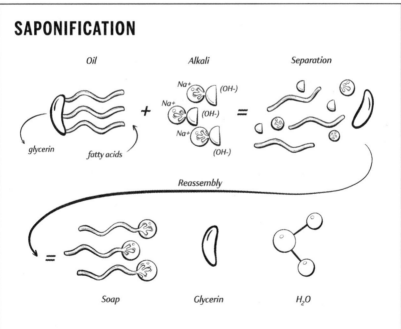

SAPONIFICATION

Oil   *Alkali*   *Separation*

glycerin   *fatty acids*   *(OH-)*

Reassembly

Soap   *Glycerin* H_2O

In the saponification, or soapmaking, reaction, two ingredients go in and three come out. Oil and alkali go in. Soap, glycerin, and water come out.

used to make liquid soap. As you'll see, none of these alkalis remain in the finished soap.

The fats and oils used in soapmaking are triglycerides. The meaning of that word hides within it. "Glyceride" refers to the glycerin molecule that forms the backbone of the oil or fat molecule. "Tri-" means three, and refers to the three fatty acids that are attached to the glycerin, making it resemble a capital E. While the glycerin is the same across types of fats or oils, there are many fatty acids, such as oleic, lauric, stearic, capric, palmitic. Fatty acids are categorized by the lengths of their carbon chains into short, medium, or long. There's been much attention of late to "medium-chain triglycerides," which are oil or fat molecules whose fatty acids contain 6–12 carbon atoms.

Sodium and potassium hydroxide are much smaller molecules made of a sodium or potassium ion connected to an oxygen-hydrogen (OH-) molecule.

During saponification, which is the reaction that produces soap, the alkali separates the fatty acids from the glycerin and also disassociates itself into the ion and hydroxide. Then everything gets rearranged. The sodium or potassium ions latch on to the fatty acids, which makes soap; the hydroxides form into water; and the glycerin is left free floating by itself. What we have left is soap, water, and glycerin. Two inputs, three outputs. Beautifully simple.

Some soapmakers drain off the glycerin to sell as a separate by-product. At Dr. Bronner's, we leave it in because glycerin works as a humectant, drawing moisture into and smoothing skin.

ORIGIN STORY:
Regenerative Organic Certified Virgin Coconut Oil

The story of Dr. Bronner's Regenerative Organic Certified® Virgin Coconut Oil is one of triumph from tragedy. In late 2004 a tsunami devastated the island nation of Sri Lanka and other lands on the rim of the Indian Ocean. Dr. Bronner's joined many other humanitarian organizations in the cleanup efforts, during which my colleague Gero Leson, our vice president of special operations, learned about the "Coconut Triangle" on the island, a region where coconuts were abundant but did not have a clear path to market.

Coconut oil is one of the primary ingredients in Dr. Bronner's Pure-Castile Soaps and most other products. We made a commitment in 2005 to source all of our major ingredients from fair trade sources but ran into a problem: there was no source big enough to supply our demand of coconut oil. This inspired a project resulting in the building of an organic and fair trade coconut oil mill, called Serendipol—Sinhalese for "blessed coconut"—near Kuliyapitiya, an hour north of the commercial metropolis Colombo in Sri Lanka. The mill has since been certified to the newer and more rigorous Regenerative Organic Certification® Silver standard.

The workers at the mill benefit from the fair trade standards of employment, guaranteeing steady and nondiscriminatory employment, fair compensation, medical benefits, school equipment for their children, and grants for personal home improvement projects. Furthermore, a team from Serendipol has supported and trained thousands of farmers in the surrounding area as they've transitioned to organic and now regenerative organic practices.

The mill produces such superb oil that we couldn't bear to hide it in the soaps. We decided to sell it as a pure food-grade oil starting in 2012.

continues

Of the many things I love about the operation at Serendipol, which I had the joy of visiting in 2014, is how all the by-products of the oil production are put to use: the husks are sold for processing into rope, mats, and erosion control; the shells are burned as fuel in the mill's boiler or turned into charcoal; the leftover seed cake becomes animal feed; and the coconut water is sold to a local bottler or used to irrigate the mill's garden.

Fair trade standards include a premium paid into a community betterment fund that has funded over 1,000 projects with over $2 million in the area around the mill. I was able to attend the dedication of a recently cleaned-out reservoir that would provide enough water to the surrounding rice farmers to grow two crops a year instead of one. I also visited a group home for girls that had established a dozen industrial sewing machines and an instructor to go with them in order to train the soon-to-graduate students in a profitable vocation. Other projects include bridges, roads, school bathrooms, critical medical equipment at a rural hospital, and electricity to remote villages.

You can read more about this project and the far-reaching benefits one business can make in Gero's book, *Honor Thy Label: Dr. Bronner's Unconventional Journey to a Clean, Green, and Ethical Supply Chain*.

RECIPES AND HOW-TOS
Produce Wash

The CDC recommends washing all produce, even types you intend to peel, so that exterior debris doesn't transfer to the edible insides during cutting or serving. If it is organic produce, a 10-second rinse under cold water, with some agitation (rubbing or scrubbing depending on its durability) to remove dirt and microorganisms, is usually sufficient.

If you feel more cleaning is needed, or if the produce is not organic, Dr. Bronner's Pure-Castile Soap and Sal Suds are both great options because they are both clean-rinsing and will leave no residues to flavor your food. The CDC has a general statement not to use dish soap on produce but this is because most dish soap leaves residues intentionally, and these would not be safe to ingest. However, residues are not a problem with these two Dr. Bronner's products. They can remove field dirt or other debris, stowaways, and wax. What they cannot do is remove systemic pesticides or herbicides that have absorbed into the skin of produce. This is why it is best to purchase organic when possible, especially for crops that tend to be more heavily doused and that can't be peeled, such as leafy greens, berries, stone fruits, and whole vegetables like broccoli and celery.

When to Wash Produce

Most produce has a protective microbiome, a film of beneficial bacteria that keeps it fresh for longer. Once you wash this off, the produce begins to wilt and decay. Therefore, it is best to wash most produce right before you are going to eat it. If you are washing further ahead of consumption, be sure to dry the food thoroughly.

The one exception to this is leafy greens, especially romaine, cabbage, chard, and kale. Not only are they sometimes crisped up by a washing, but this is also a great way to set yourself up for eating success by having washed greens at the ready.

HOW TO WASH PRODUCE

Sal Suds—one drop in a bowl of water OR
Pure-Castile Soap—one dash (approximately ¼ teaspoon or
1.24 ml) in a bowl of water OR a dollop of soap from your
foaming hand pump for a single item

1. Dunk the produce in the sudsy water, or rub the foam or spray around the surfaces, and rinse. Do not let produce sit in water or it may absorb the water and become soggy. For a single item, one drop of Pure-Castile Soap or Sal Suds, or one squirt from my foaming pump is plenty for an easy scrub and rinse.

2. For multiple items, fill a bowl or a clean sink with cold water and a few drops of Sal Suds or Pure-Castile Soap. Dunk the produce and swish it to be sure all sides get clean and the dirt has a chance to loosen and fall.

3. Transfer the produce to a colander and rinse thoroughly in cold water.

CLEANING THE MICROWAVE

Lemons are nature's offering to the world of cleaning. They're acidic, they're spongy, and they smell super. I have a dwarf lemon tree, which I planted for edible purposes, but I probably actually use it more for cleaning. If lemons are not readily available, take note of the alternatives I mention.

The acidity of the lemons is at work here. Acidity loosens the baked-on grime beautifully. If ever you feel ineffective in whatever your day contains, go clean your microwave with a lemon. You'll feel like you have superpowers.

1 lemon, quartered

1. Place the cut lemon on the microwave plate and heat for 2 minutes.

2. Keep the microwave door closed for an additional 5 minutes.

3. Open the microwave and wipe down.

ALTERNATIVES: Use a cup with ½ cup (120 ml) white vinegar in ½ cup (120 ml) water, or even a cup of water alone. The steam will still work wonders.

CLEANING THE GARBAGE DISPOSAL

½ lemon, thinly sliced

1. With the disposal off, put the slices down the drain. With cold water running, turn on the disposal. Run the disposal until you don't hear any more grinding.

2. The underside of the rubber flange at the entrance to your drain may be another source of malodorous smells. Take a soapy dish brush or cloth and wash the underside of this flange.

ALTERNATIVES: If you don't have lemons, freeze vinegar in small cubes and grind them in the disposal.

DEODORIZING SMELLY CUTTING BOARDS

1 lemon, cut in half
Table salt

Sprinkle the cut side of the lemon liberally with the salt. Scrub the surface of the cutting board with the salty lemon. Set the board with its lemony salt paste (yum?) out in the sun. Once the paste dries, wash the lemon and salt off the cutting board.

CLEAN YOUR FRIDGE INSIDE AND OUT

Cleaning the fridge not only makes the fridge more sanitary, it makes the food in it look so much more appetizing!

1. Start with the outside. Vacuum beneath and behind your fridge to improve energy efficiency, cooling efficacy, and maybe even safety since the buildup of dust and cobwebs can cause a buildup of heat. Pull the fridge out from against the wall and unplug it. Use the hose of a vacuum fitted with a brush attachment to vacuum under

the fridge and the coils on the back. You may have a removable grate on the bottom that you can wash thoroughly in the sink with soapy water. A few drops of Sal Suds or Pure-Castile Soap are perfect for this.

2. While the fridge is pulled out, mop beneath it. If you're not already mopping the floor, you can just spray the floor with the GIY All-Purpose Cleaning Spray and go over it with a damp mop or cloth. Clean the front, sides, and top with the GIY All-Purpose Cleaning Spray and wipe with a damp cloth. Dry with a dry cloth for the best finish.

3. To clean the inside of the fridge, it really works best if you take all the food out. You'll see what you have, and you'll get the best clean. If shelves and drawers are removable, take them out and wash them in a sink of soapy water with a small squirt of Sal Suds or Pure-Castile Soap. Do not put cold glass shelves directly in warm or hot soapy water. The heat difference could crack them. If shelves are not removable, wash them with a soapy cloth or with the GIY All-Purpose Cleaning Spray followed by a damp cloth. Vacuum out the crumbs in the back bottom of your fridge. Use the GIY All-Purpose Cleaning Spray and a damp cloth to wipe down all interior surfaces of the fridge. Even the walls and ceiling of the fridge build up grime from the humidity and food fumes. Dry surfaces and shelves thoroughly and replace shelves and food.

4. To clean the freezer, transfer items into the fridge or a cooler. Using a warm cloth, wipe down the freezer and dry before moisture refreezes. Work in sections if need be. Don't use the vacuum in the freezer because ice crystals become liquid and can damage the vacuum components.

5. If your ice doesn't get used up regularly, dump it out and start a fresh batch. Replace freezer items in the freezer. (Make a catalog of what you have so that you can incorporate it in your meal plans. Somehow this feels like free food!)

6. Plug the refrigerator back in. Push the fridge back into place, being careful not to crush the water line.

DISHWASHING

Hand dishwashing with Dr. Bronner's is another choose-your-own adventure. I've got lots of options for you! Both the Sal Suds and the Pure-Castile Soap work great on dishes. Sal Suds is a little better at grease cutting and is unaffected by hard water. Both are readily biodegradable, so whether your drain empties to the sewer, a septic system, or even a gray water system, the products will break down quickly and pose no harm to the environment.

SAL SUDS: One drop per pot or plate, a small squirt in a sink of water.

PURE-CASTILE LIQUID SOAP: A couple drops per pot or plate, a slightly larger squirt in a sink of water.

FOAMING PUMP DISPENSER: A squirt or two of soap from a foaming pump dispenser for a single item.

PURE-CASTILE BAR SOAP: Rub your dish brush on a bar of the Pure-Castile Soap (this works great with a palm brush, which can be stored neatly in a shaving brush holder). Or grate 1 tablespoon bar soap and dissolve in a sink of warm or hot water.

SOAP CREAM MADE WITH PURE-CASTILE BAR SOAP (PAGE 160): Swish 3 tablespoons in a sink of water.

Alternatives to Sponges

Sponges often top the lists of "dirtiest objects in your house." It makes sense that they would. We wipe all manner of things with them and then they sit damp and sometimes warm, which is the perfect breeding ground for all things growing. A better option is something that is washable and reusable. Loofah sponges (which are sliced sections of one of nature's strangest fruits), genuine Swedish dishcloths, and walnut scrubbers are excellent options. I like to use crocheted dishcloths made from 100 percent cotton yarn. You can make your own or find them at a craft shop. It is best to use a clean washcloth daily or swap it out after an icky cleanup.

CLEANING THE SINK

Spray with the GIY All-Purpose Cleaning Spray or a few drops of Sal Suds or Pure-Castile Soap and then sprinkle on some baking soda. Scrub with a dish brush and rinse well. Dry the sink for maximum sparkle. The GIY Soft Scrub is another excellent option here.

The Versatility of Bar Soap

Bar soap sales are rising significantly because plastic is at the forefront of consumers' environmental concerns and budgetary considerations are right behind them. At Dr. Bronner's, sales of Pure-Castile Bar Soap have grown unhesitatingly around 10 percent annually for quite a number of years now. While in part I think there is a certain retro allure to the humble bar, its paper wrappers and superconcentrated soap content meet many needs.

The Dr. Bronner's Pure-Castile Bar Soap is far more versatile than it is given credit for being. Almost all of the liquid soap uses and dilutions are possible with the bar soap. The same chemistry that powers the liquid soap powers the bar. The same surfactant action, the same emulsification, the same micelle formation. It's as simple, effective, and clean-rinsing as its liquid counterpart. I bring it up here in The Kitchen because some of these uses require some kitchen gadgetry. Here are a few ways to use the Dr. Bronner's Pure-Castile Bar Soap other than your daily shower:

+ Hand-washing delicates: Get them wet and then rub them lightly with bar soap. Soak, swish, and rinse, and off you go.
+ Fabric stain management: Wet the stain. Rub the bar soap on the spot. Let it sit until full laundering.
+ Dog washing: I discuss dog washing in greater detail on page 200, but imagine that you can massage in the bar soap instead of the liquid.
+ Any cleaning that uses a brush: A dish brush, a scrub brush, a fingernail brush—run the brush over the soap bar to pick up a nice amount for your cleaning task.
+ Cleaning makeup brushes: Wet the makeup brush. Run it lightly over the bar. Massage in the suds. Rinse well and dry.
+ Shaving with a brush: Cut a section of bar soap to fit in a shaving cup. Lather up a good foam with a shaving brush. Apply to skin and shave. Rinse.
+ Cut bar soap: Cutting a bar of soap into smaller sections is helpful when traveling, sharing, or dedicating a portion to a particular use. This works

continues

best with a fresh bar, given that an older bar may crumble. Use a sharp knife and a cutting board. Carefully cut the bar into two to five sections.

+ Grated bar soap: Grate soap with a kitchen box grater or with a hand rotary cheese grater. Dissolve the gratings in a sink for washing dishes, in a tub for a nice soak, or to make a Powdered Laundry Soap (page 121),

+ Create a semiliquid soap, which I've dubbed Soap Cream: Soak half of a cubed bar of Dr. Bronner's Pure-Castile Soap in 2 cups of water overnight and then blend it on low. This makes a foamy gel that you can dilute it to make the GIY All-Purpose Cleaning Spray or any of my liquid GIY housecleaning solutions.

+ Drawer, luggage, or shoe freshener: Put a whole or a slice of bar soap in a tissue or mesh bag and tuck into a drawer, cabinet, suitcase, or shoes to keep things smelling fresh.

There's been some chatter of concern that bar soaps harbor germs, but they don't. Enough people have asked that it's been studied formally. Both a 1965 study and a 1988 study verified that bar soaps do not transfer germs from one surface or set of hands to the next.[58]

Kitchen Surfaces

Keep a spray bottle of GIY All-Purpose Cleaning Spray (page 91), made with either the Sal Suds or Pure-Castile Soap, in your kitchen. This is all I use for every surface: counters (mine are quartzite), backsplashes (mine are glass tile), cabinets (mine are painted wood), appliances (mine are brushed stainless), and even walls, doors, and light switches. I'll dive into a few in specific because they tend to raise the most questions, but as a summary statement: clean your kitchen surfaces with the GIY All-Purpose Cleaning Spray. Spray the surfaces and wipe with a damp cloth. Dry with a dry cloth for maximum shine.

CLEANING STONE, CERAMIC, OR SYNTHETIC TILE

Though all stone may feel hard, some stones are actually harder than others. This matters when it comes to cleaning. Too acidic of a cleaner, like vinegar with a pH of roughly 2 to 3, used repeatedly on a soft stone can dull or pit it. The acid is actually dissolving minerals in the stone. A scratchy cloth can etch or scratch soft stones. While some people call this "character" in soapstone, it can go a little too far.

In case your mind has just run to, "I have no idea what kind of stone I've got! It's whatever the place came with!" I've got you covered.

A mild, near-neutral cleaner (such as the GIY All-Purpose Cleaning Spray made from Dr. Bronner's Pure-Castile Soap, page 91, or Sal Suds is safe for any stone when used as follows)

1. Absorb any spilled liquids by blotting (so as not to spread any potential stain). Wipe up any crumbs by lightly brushing with a dry cloth.

2. Spray with the GIY All-Purpose Cleaning Spray.

3. Wipe with a damp cloth. If you see bubbles remain on the surface, rinse the cloth and wipe again.

4. Dry with a soft, dry cloth.

5. Alternatively, for floors, mop with mopping solution. Absorb any standing water left on the floor.

HERE'S THE COMMANDMENT FOR STONE: No scrubbies. No powders. Not even soft scrub gels, which are powders suspended in liquids. All of these can etch that surface. Be assured that soap is enough. It will remove the grime and germs—yes, even if there was raw meat or eggs—and leave behind a clean surface.

Furthermore, follow your manufacturer's advice on sealing your stone, too. I once ignored that part because I thought nothing could hurt granite. After a crack encircled my kitchen sink, I now have a new countertop and an emptier bank account.

Stainless Steel

Stainless steel is a terrible secret keeper. Whether you have the more common brushed stainless on your appliances or the polished, it relentlessly reveals fingerprints, nose prints, or any other prints that have dared to touch it.

Stainless steel, which is an alloy of iron, chromium, and other metals, gets its brushed look by being polished with a moderate grit belt or wheel. This gives it a subtle luster instead of the bright shine of polished stainless, as well as a directionality, or grain. Though the surface feels smooth to our hand, it is in fact finely grooved. These grooves are what hold on to grease (i.e., fingerprints) so very well.

CLEANING STAINLESS STEEL

Always wipe in the direction of the grain. Keeping your strokes in the direction of the grain cleans them out better and doesn't fight the directionality.

FOR STOVETOPS, OVENS, TOASTERS, ETC.:

Wait until the surface is completely cool. This is partially for your safety and partially for your sanity. When stainless is warm, it's like washing a car in full sun: the water will evaporate before you have a chance to wipe it and will leave behind soap and mineral deposits. That's nothing but frustrating.

FOR LIGHT CLEANING:

When there's merely dust and a few fingerprints: spray a vinegar solution of half white vinegar/half water and wipe with your damp cloth.

FOR MODERATE CLEANING:

When there are many fingerprints and a bit of light cooking residue: spray the GIY All-Purpose Cleaning Spray and wipe with a comfortably hot, damp cloth

FOR HEAVY CLEANING:

When facing stubborn, baked-on cooking residues on stovetops (for me this means burned splatters from my annual apple butter–making marathon), try one of these techniques, in order of increasing intensity:

+ Lay a very hot, wet cloth over the grime, taking care not to burn yourself, and let it sit until cool. Then wipe it up.
+ Sprinkle baking soda, which adds a very gentle scrub and is not sharp enough to scratch stainless, lightly on your rag and rub moderately in the direction of the grain.
+ For the toughest grime, make a thin paste with baking soda and Dr. Bronner's Pure-Castile Soap or Sal Suds. Spread this on the crud, let it sit for 10 minutes, wipe off, and rinse.
+ Rinse all cleaning agents off your stainless with a damp cloth. Residues will show.

✦ Dry the surface thoroughly with a dry cloth. Continue to wipe in the direction of the grain until completely dry. Dried water spots or lines will mar the shine afterward.

What to Avoid with Stainless Steel

✦ Abrasive cleaners, such as scouring powders or anything with a scouring agent, can scratch polished or brushed steel. Even abrasive tools, such as steel wool, stiff brushes, plastic scrubbies, or rough sponges, can mar these finishes.

✦ Cleaners that leave residues will shine like a beacon in the night, and not a good one. Use clean rinsing products only.

✦ Bleach, or any cleaner containing bleach, is made of sodium hypochlorite, which can accumulate in the grooves of the surface and break down the chromium oxide of the steel. Over time, this results in corrosion.

✦ Salt is bad for stainless steel for two reasons. Dry salt is an abrasive that will scratch the surface. But even if the salt is dissolved in water, the chloride ions can also corrode the surface.

Cleaning the Oven

Conventional oven cleaners are problematic because they are so corrosive. They are just behind drain cleaner in their gunk-eating power.

Sodium hydroxide is common in oven cleaner. I know this one well because it is used in the soapmaking process. None ever remains in the final product, and it's a good thing. Sodium hydroxide, or caustic soda or lye, is an extremely alkaline substance with a pH of 14. Remember that the pH scale stops at 14, so this is very extreme. In oven cleaner, the sodium hydroxide is in the formulation so that it can eat through that gunk coating your oven. And then it can go down your drain and eat stuff in the waterways, causing great harm to habitats and disrupting the pH balance of septic systems.

There are several simple, cheap, far safer ways to clean your oven. The first step is to remove any loose matter: any crumbs or tidbits or loose ash. Sometimes I even use my vacuum hose. This is the mechanical cleaning needed in order for the thermal or chemical means to be effective.

Self-Cleaning Ovens

There are some pros and cons to using the self-cleaning feature on your oven. It certainly is convenient, cleaning the oven at the press of a button or the turn of a knob. Plus, this method does not use any harsh chemicals. On the downside, it uses a lot of energy to get up to the 600+ degrees required and maintain it for several hours. It also can emit acrid fumes, though there is no solid research either way on the amount of fumes emitted or the dangers they pose. At the very least, if you use your oven's self-cleaning feature, turn on any available vents, such as the range hood; open the windows; and keep the air circulating with house or ceiling fans. Be sure to remove the oven racks beforehand and clean those separately. You also will need to wipe out the ash afterward. Anyone with respiratory ailments might want to head out for a few hours.

LEMON OR VINEGAR STEAM

You'll need lemons and a pot with a lid for this one. The oven stays off, or else it will vent all this lovely steam outside.

3 to 5 lemons, quartered
1 cup water

1. Remove all but one oven rack. Fill a 4-quart stove pot with the lemons and water. Cover the pot and heat the contents on the stove to simmer. Allow it to simmer, covered, for 15 minutes or so until the lemons are soft. Keep the lid on. Transfer the pot to the oven, remove the lid, and immediately shut the oven.

   Alternatively, fill the pot with equal amounts vinegar and water, cover, and bring it to a steady simmer. Then transfer it to the oven, remove the lid, and shut the oven.

   Alternatively, the pot can be prepared in the microwave, using a covered microwave-safe casserole dish.

2. Keep the oven closed for at least 1 hour. Then open the oven and wipe off loosened crud with a damp cloth. If it needs a little more action, use the GIY All-Purpose Cleaning Spray (page 91) and baking soda to scour.

BAKING SODA PASTE

For the remaining stubborn burned spots, or if your oven is generally clean and only has some stubborn burns, make a paste out of baking soda and water.

Baking soda
Water

1. Add just enough water to the baking soda to make a spreadable paste, mixing it with a fork to break up the lumps. Spread this on the burned spots. Let it sit overnight. Yep, overnight. Time is your helper here.

2. In the morning, scrape off the paste with a plastic scraper and throw the paste in the trash. Use the GIY All-Purpose Cleaning Spray (page 91) with a little more baking soda to wipe off any remaining spots.

Cleaning the Stovetop

Whether you have a gas, electric, or induction stovetop and the surface is made from stainless steel, coated ceramic, enamel, or glass, the Pure-Castile Soap and Sal Suds keep them sparkling. As with grime anywhere, the sooner you tackle cleaning it, the better. However, I definitely have had my share of stubborn messes.

1. Clean off loose material.

2. Spray with the GIY All-Purpose Cleaning Spray (page 91) and wipe with a damp cloth.

3. If burned-on material remains, lay a washcloth over the area and pour enough hot water onto it to saturate the cloth. Let the cloth sit for 10 minutes or until it is cool enough to handle. Scrub away. Use a plastic scraper on the remaining grime.

Seasoning and Cleaning Cast Iron and Stone Bakeware

The first step to good ware care is seasoning, which does not refer to your favorite garlic and herb blend, but rather to creating a layer over the surface that provides a nonstick coating and, for cast iron, protection against rust. The fancy term for this layer is polymerization, which means that through extended heat, oil bonds to the surface. Most oils can work for this, though you'll certainly find devotees of one oil over another. Dr. Bronner's Virgin Coconut Oil works well and is what I use. Some cast iron and stoneware come preseasoned, which is handy, but you still may need to reseason the pan at some point.

HOW TO SEASON CAST IRON

1. Heat the oven to 425°F (218°C).

2. Coat the cookware with a thin layer of coconut oil. More is not better here; a thick layer makes it more difficult to achieve the chemical reaction, and the resulting coating is more likely to flake off.

3. Place the cookware upside down in the oven. You may want to place the item on a rimmed baking sheet to prevent oil drips onto your oven floor.

4. Leave for 1 hour and then turn the oven off, but leave the door closed until it is fully cool, around 2 hours. If the surface is still tacky, repeat the oven process.

HOW TO SEASON STONEWARE

Follow the directions for cast iron, except set the oven to 400°F (200°C) and bake the stoneware for only 30 minutes.

HOW TO CLEAN SEASONED CAST IRON OR STONEWARE

1. To keep from removing the seasoning layer, clean cast iron and bakeware primarily with heat and mechanical action. This means use hot water and something abrasive, which could be a stiff brush, a scraper, or coarse salt. If you need a little more cleaning power, a small amount of Sal Suds or Pure-Castile Soap is a mild enough cleanser not to disturb the seasoning.

2. Dry the item thoroughly, which is particularly important for cast iron not to rust. If your oven is still warm, place the washed bakeware in the oven to dry fully.

HOW TO SEASON WOODEN SPOONS

Sand spoons if needed. Wash in soapy water and let dry thoroughly. Coat with a thin film of coconut oil. Bake at 375°F (190°C) for 2 minutes. Remove and let cool.

HOW TO SEASON CUTTING BOARDS

In a double boiler, combine 1 cup (240 ml) liquid coconut oil with ¼ cup (60 ml) melted beeswax. Stir to form a smooth, thick paste. Rub into the cutting board with a circular motion until the board will not absorb more. Wipe off excess and let air dry.

Ask Lisa

Q Does Dr. Bronner's Pure-Castile Soap contain chemicals?

A I always have to remind myself to answer the questioner and not the question. The answer to the question is yes because soap is a chemical. But usually the person wants to know if the soap contains anything toxic, to which I can answer no.

Q Can I use Dr. Bronner's Pure-Castile Soap or Sal Suds in a dishwasher?

A No. Though I've heard many individual claims to the contrary, no Dr. Bronner's product works universally well in dishwashers. I have never been able to get it to work for me, and the experts universally decry using detergents that weren't formulated for dishwashers. My brother tried it and ended up with a bubble party on his kitchen floor. The kids were thrilled. Dishwasher formulations are always no-suds, which is a different type of detergent. If you've spent any time around the Pure-Castile Soap and Sal Suds, you know they both make suds.

Q Will the soap clog my pipes or cause drains to drain slowly?

A No. The Pure-Castile Soap on its own will not clog your pipes, even in hard water. However, if you have combined the Pure-Castile Soap with substances like Epsom salts (magnesium sulfate) or vinegar, you have created a gunk that can clog pipes.

CHAPTER 5
THE OFFICE

Every generation must find a way to leave the planet, leave this little spaceship, Earth, this little piece of real estate, a little better than we found it —a little cleaner, a little greener, and a little more peaceful.
—CONGRESSMAN JOHN LEWIS

In 2012 I lost my fear and found my public voice.

The turning point happened one evening when I was sitting in my car outside the KUSI television newsroom in San Diego. I was there to appear live on the evening news to present the case for why genetically modified foods (or GMOs) should be labeled, a position with which few public voices agreed. I was speaking on behalf of the "Yes on 37—California Right to Know Genetically Engineered Food Act" campaign.

David had become passionate about the issue when he learned most engineering was not done to boost nutrition or yield but rather to boost resistance to herbicides, resulting in chemically saturated crops. He was heavily involved in the campaign and had called me a few months prior to say that "Yes on 37" needed someone to present our case before editorial review boards and news outlets. Would I consider doing it?

Of course I would not! That sort of thing is for real people. I was just a mom. One who spent days stepping on Legos, cheering on my son's soccer team—the Snot Rockets—and considered it a good day if I was able to brush my teeth AND my hair. But most of all, one who stoutly avoided conflict and who shivered uncontrollably when speaking into a microphone.

But the campaign was small and seriously underfunded. The very definition of grassroots. On the opposition was Big Ag, with recognizable names like Dow and Monsanto, who outspent the "Yes" side by a factor of five.

There weren't loads of options for who could go speak publicly, and they certainly couldn't pay anyone. Other than fear, I didn't have a better reason to say no. I believed in the cause, and I didn't want to disappoint my brother. So, I said yes.

Fear was the focus of my thoughts as I sat in my car outside the studio in the fading light. But why was I afraid? It was highly unlikely that I would be physically harmed in a newsroom on live television. A question surfaced in my head, like a little tap on my consciousness, "What do you think these people will do to you?"

There, in that moment, the humanity of the people inside the building struck me. They were people. They likely disagreed with me about GMOs, but in other matters we were similar. They were people trying to do the best they could, the best way they knew how, taking care of themselves and their loved ones, just as I was. We were about to cross paths over this one issue, but other than that, we likely could have a fine conversation about our pets or our plans for the weekend.

And there it was. That obvious simple truth. Disagreements are not the end of either of us. Even when we disagree, even on something important, we have so much more in common.

I went on into that news station. I clipped on my microphone. I walked on to the platform and sat in the chair and answered their questions. Every step a conscious decision. I made my points. I don't know if I was persuasive. For my personal journey, though, it was a turning point. I stopped being afraid to speak.

My grandfather's life message finally found resonance in me: we are all "brothers and sisters on God's Spaceship Earth," as he would say, whether in a newsroom or through a computer or on the street. And no one always agrees with their brothers and sisters, but we are each bigger than any one topic. It gave context to the work that I do and to my place within my family legacy.

Growing up, I didn't know what to make of my grandfather. As children, my brothers and I would listen in quiet bewilderment to his Moral ABC, his manual for life, the message he committed his life to and put on the label of soap bottles. If you examine a bottle of Dr. Bronner's Pure-Castile Peppermint Soap today, you'll be reading what I grew up hearing: tenets for living and connecting with all people. "1st: If I'm not for me, who am I? Nobody! 2nd: Yet, if I'm only for me, what am I? Nothing!" Jumping a bit, "5th: Whatever unites mankind is better than whatever divides us!"

The most time I spent with my grandfather was the summer I was 18. For a month, I worked in the office and lived in a room above his patio that was surrounded by avocado trees and weaver spiders. My grandfather was far into his decline from Parkinson's disease, bedridden and with 24/7 nursing care. He had immense trouble expressing himself at this point. Looking back, I wish I'd had the presence of mind and imagination to engage with him in ways he could still manage, such as by playing music or reading to him the poetry he loved.

Instead, I thought of all the questions I had about his life that he could no longer answer. What was it like in Germany during the First World War and between the wars? What anti-Semitism did you experience? What kind of relationship did you have with your mother and sisters? Did you have any regrets about leaving Germany when you did? Are you proud of your German Jewish heritage? What was your relationship like with Paula (my grandmother)?

As I look back at that time, I realize these questions were not critical. The time for questions had passed. More important was being present with him and helping him be at peace. I wish I had connected with him as he was able.

Now these decades later, many a late night finds me in my office, exploring our family history, piecing together the stories and lives. My nondescript brown faux-leather chair is a magical cockpit to take me to far distant places and times. The surge in recently digitized archives reveals document after pivotal document chronicling turning points in our generations. My great-great-grandfather's 1858 authorization certificate to become a master soapmaker in Laupheim, Germany; the ship manifests tracking my grandfather's emigration from Hamburg, Germany, to New York in 1929; censuses showing where he was, who he was with, how he was living, and what he was doing as though I were reading a diary; my great-grandparents' visas finally permitting them to leave Germany dated December 5, 1941, which they never had a chance to use; passenger lists with their names among those transported from Heilbronn to the Theresienstadt concentration camp; their death certificates handwritten by the camp physicians; the death certificates of each of my grandfather's four wives. From this small room, I have explored and connected deeply with my family members as their voices speak to me from these records. (For readers who want to dive into the history a bit more, please see page 226.)

ORIGIN STORY:
Dr. Bronner's Pure-Castile Liquid Soap Scents

My grandfather began selling his family's Pure-Castile Liquid Soap in the United States in 1955 with the Peppermint Pure-Castile Liquid Soap. Staunchly defiant of the country's surge toward "better living through chemistry," Dr. Bronner refused to use artificial fragrance or artificial anything in his soaps. Essential oils were all he ever used, and he didn't skimp.

Still to this day, if people know only one scent of Dr. Bronner's Pure-Castile Soap, they know the Peppermint, with its royal blue label. The zest! The tingle! It's been described as a snowman hug, a York Peppermint Pattie in your underwear, the love child of an apothecary and a magician. Still the company's best seller by far, the Peppermint wakes

continues

you up and cools you down with its dual mint blend of *Mentha piperita* and *Mentha arvensis*. Peppermint's sensation of coolness comes from the abundant menthol in peppermint oil, which stimulates the same nerve receptors in our skin that sense cold.[59] Since roughly half of peppermint oil is menthol, that's a hefty dose of epidermal trickery. Peppermint was the favorite scent of my dad, Jim, and is my mom, Trudy's, go-to in the summer.

For two decades the Peppermint had the stage to itself, until my grandfather debuted the Almond, with its emerald green label, in 1975. I'll be forever grateful. My favorite (and my mom's favorite in the colder months) for personal care, the Almond is mellow and soothing, like a cup of tea in a comfy chair. The perfect way to ease into or out of the day. The Almond is ultimate companion soap: it blends well with everything. Citrus and Almond, Peppermint and Almond, Rose and Almond. It's a friend to all. Maybe it's my favorite because I aspire to the same thing.

The Eucalyptus and Lavender Pure-Castile Soap scents both arrived in 1978. Like a pair of fraternal twins, they have decidedly different profiles—wild versus cultured, adventurous versus serene. The brown-labeled Eucalyptus is woodsy, earthy, fresh, reminiscent of forest wildness. Eucalyptus oil is naturally high in eucalyptol, which has a similar cooling feel to mint. Though a lesser-known scent in the Bronner's lineup, it is Mike's favorite. My dad blended the Eucalyptus with the Peppermint to make his Euco-Peppo Bear Wash. As far as I know, he never used it on a bear, though it was all he used to wash our dogs.

Where Eucalyptus is untamed, Lavender is rich with cultivation. Refined but passionate, our Lavender is no flimsy flash, but is lush and spiced, opening the senses and elevating the spirit. Long reputed as a calming scent, lavender penetrates deeply. More than other synthetic scents, true lavender has been done the biggest disservice by artificial fragrances found in many products, which bear so little resemblance to the complexity of the real thing. Dr. Bronner's Lavender comes from a blend of two essential oils, lavender and lavandin. This was the favorite of my dad's older brother, my inimitable Uncle Ralph, and is what I give to new parents in my circles—to bring calm to both parent and child alike.

The Baby Unscented, arriving in 1979, was originally labeled in light pink but later changed to light blue. Not only does the Baby Unscented lack essential oils, but it also has double the amount in ratio of olive oil. While saponified olive oil does not lather as copiously as saponified coconut oil, it is more soothing to the skin. This makes it the go-to soap for two groups: those who want no scent either by preference or because of sensitivities and those who want the freedom of adding their own essential oil blends to the soap.

David brought the Tea Tree Pure-Castile, with its bright orange label, to the lineup in 1998. Research was pouring in about this native Australian plant's success in the treatment of acne, fungal infections, and general antimicrobial action.[60] A clarifying and therapeutic scent, the Tea Tree Pure-Castile resides in both my bathroom and my housecleaning cabinet. Tea Tree combined with the Eucalyptus is a compellingly clean scent for anyone who thinks that green cleaners lack that convincing aromatic punch of conventional cleaners.

The last two scents were brought in by Mike: the Rose in 2006 and the Citrus in 2008. The Rose, with its deep pink label, is a rich blend of floral essential oils. It brings to mind an abundant summer garden, exuberant in blooms, with lazy drunken bees bumbling from flower to flower. Sweet and plush, the Rose Pure-Castile is welcoming and one I often keep in my guest bathroom.

The light orange–labeled Citrus, with its blend of sweet orange, lemon, and lime essential oils, is my backup favorite and my top choice for housecleaning. I keep this happy scent by my kitchen sink, and it is what I'll use in the shower when I want to change things up a bit. It is fresh and bright and sunny, reminiscent of the most perfect warm spring day.

GOING GREEN IN THE OFFICE

My office is also where I interact daily with incredibly diverse people who constantly remind me how much life experience we share. My blog and social channels connect with people from every corner and every realm, and what I've found is that taking care of ourselves and our loved ones and our spaces is a great commonality. Despite potential differing opinions on other topics, we all live some version of a sleep/wake, work/play/rest rhythm in our days. We bathe, we dress, we eat, we clean, we live in some space. Regardless of whom we vote for, whom we worship, or whom we marry, we likely brushed our teeth this morning, or at least we know we should have. People are endlessly interesting and incredibly resilient. As I learned that night at KUSI, people are not to be feared. People are beautiful.

RECIPES AND HOW-TOS
Setting Up the Office for Productivity and Well-Being

The time you spend setting up your work space for focus and productivity will come back to you abundantly over the years. This is a highly personalized process. What works for me will likely not be the same as what works for the next person. If you met me, David, Mike, and Michael and then saw our offices, you could probably match our personalities to our work space very easily. Take a moment to think about how you work best. Here's what I've prioritized for mine.

A GOOD CHAIR: I put this one first for a reason. A good chair makes or breaks a workday. Prioritize support and comfort over style or color. This is one item I recommend putting some money toward. It is an investment. To skimp on the chair will likely cost money in chiropractic or massage expenses down the road. Consider if a standing desk would work better for you.

TASK LIGHTING: Regardless of the ambient light in the room, bring in a desk lamp. It brings warmth to the area, especially if the overhead light is fluorescent or overly white. It can help focus your attention on the task before you. For me, since my computer sits against a dark corner, it helps reduce eye strain by spreading the light.

A GREEN PLANT: In the midst of the fabricated surfaces of an office, a green plant reminds me of the larger world and connects me to another living thing. And though I mean a live plant, though if the idea of a live one is overwhelming, an artificial plant would still be a reminder of good things growing.

SOMETHING INSPIRATIONAL: There is huge variety in this category. I have a memo board where I tuck favorite quotes and pictures. It's a little messy but I love it. Michael has a few small neatly framed family photos—more tidy and minimalist than mine. David's space is filled with collected artwork from friends, each a memory. Mike has elegantly framed watercolors from Japan.

A COASTER: Even if the desk is some impervious surface, I like to have a coaster because it reminds me where to set my drink, out of range of an accidental bump. It also gives my drink (for me that's water, tea, or coffee) a home, an intentional place so that it doesn't look so messy.

A BED FOR FURRY COWORKERS: This is irrelevant if you don't have four-footed coworkers, but for me this is essential. If I don't provide a bed of some sort, my cats will make themselves at home on my lap or my keyboard. Both spots are quite distracting.

A PEN HOLDER AND NOTEPAD ON THE DESK: Essential to capture galloping thoughts.

A TAH-DAH NOTEBOOK: Take my idea from the bedroom and bring it into the office. How often do you get to the end of your workday and wonder where the day went and what you got done? The Tah-Dah list records what you accomplished, big and small, and can even work as a time tracker. This can help budget time better and proves that something did get done, even if it was not what was planned.

Office Cleaning Routine in Five Steps

The office may not look as in need of cleaning as, say, the bathroom or kitchen. For the most part, messy and icky things don't happen in the office. No cooking, bathing, cutting raw meat. Or at least not in my office. But there are three key office aspects that need to be dealt with regularly: dust, air pollutants, and oft-touched objects.

1. **Dust surfaces and electronics** with a slightly damp microfiber cloth. Unplug electronics before cleaning. You don't need a dusting spray packed with chemicals; a damp cloth is sufficient to remove smudges on screens. Always clean with the least intensive method needed, and water is just that. Blow dust out of keyboards with compressed air.

2. **Clean keyboards and touchscreens** by spraying a damp cloth with the GIY All-Purpose Cleaning Spray (page 91) and wiping surfaces. Don't spray electronics directly and don't get them excessively wet. There is mixed advice on disinfecting touch screens with alcohol, because it can degrade the oleophilic coating on the screens. Refer to the manufacturer's advice. Certain UV light cleaning devices that enclose small electronics can also be effective, but do research on which ones work well.

3. **Wash doorknobs, landlines, light switches, and other oft-touched nonelectronic objects** with the GIY All-Purpose Cleaning Spray (page 91) and a damp microfiber cloth.

4. **Dust mop or vacuum the floor.** Dust hard to reach areas with regularity; dust accumulation anywhere harbors mites and contaminants.

5. **Clean the air** by opening windows or running a high-quality air purifier.

Office Tidiness in Five Steps

"Clean" and "tidy" are not the same thing. Both are important, but while cleanliness affects our physical health, tidiness affects our spirit and our schedule. An untidy space burdens the mind—a phalanx of undone tasks constantly before us—and makes finding something take a lot longer. I work much better in a tidy space, but I am not naturally a tidy person. I have to be intentional about maintaining my space. Here are some habits that have helped me.

1. **Set a 15-minute timer at the beginning of your office work to tidy.** This is when you take care of all the stuff that has accumulated since you last were in your office—the mail that's arrived, the papers the kids brought home, the stuff that mysteriously shows up on your desk. These 15 minutes are for tasks that take less than 1 minute each—file, shred, recycle, say yes or no. If something needs a longer email written, a phone call made, an item ordered online, or anything that takes longer than 1 minute, set it aside and write the item on a to-do list. (Schedule time later for the to-do list.)

2. **File or shred papers immediately.** Filing or shredding a document takes less than a minute—far less. Do not put these in piles to file or shred later. Those piles become huge and messy and daunting, and then you wonder if that was your shredding pile or your filing pile, and you better go back through it to make sure.

3. **Have a spot for "active" items.** This is a basket or upright file for papers related to an in-process task. I don't want to file them away yet, but they shouldn't sit out on the desk to clutter and get messed up. Examples are plans and receipts for an ongoing house project, travel documents for an upcoming trip, or bills awaiting payment.

4. **Have homes for all items.** Keeping office supplies on your desk sounds handy, but it is too easy for them to become visual clutter. Is it really that much harder to get your stapler out of a drawer when you need it? This keeps your field of vision clear and helps you focus on the task at hand. My exceptions are pens and a notepad, as mentioned above.

5. **Set an alarm for 5 minutes before your work time will end.** I have had to have stern talks with myself about this one. I let the end of the day sneak up on me, even though I know what the boundary is. It's not a surprise—it happens every day. I either need to go pick up a kid or head out to an appointment or start dinner. If I don't anticipate this end time, then I have to leap from my task, leaving everything out and easy to mess up, and unable to note where I was so that I can pick it back up the next day. It's so much better when I set an alarm for 5 minutes before that time to wrap up the day: charge devices, put away cords or books or papers, take my coffee cup to the kitchen, set items back in their place.

Essential Oils in the Office

While I'm not remotely qualified to dive into the therapeutic benefits of various essential oils, I can however talk about how much I like them and how I use them. You already know I use them to personalize my GIY concoctions, but I also like to have them around while I'm working. They connect me to the bigger picture and give me context for the task at hand. Remember that our scent recognition, emotions, and memory are stored together in the brain, which makes scents extremely transportive and even transformative.

For me, peppermint and lavender essential oils are the best of coworkers. Peppermint for when I'm dragging through the day and need a boost. Lavender for when the day is dragging me and I need a break. My easiest go-tos are the several Dr. Bronner's product lines that use both of these. I usually just grab one of these.

ORGANIC HAND SANITIZER: Spritz the back of the neck and even down the shirt for a refreshing pick-me-up. Spritz the air for an instant room lift. Gotta love those "off-label" uses!

ORGANIC HAND & BODY LOTION: Massage into the back of the neck and shoulders for a midday reset.

GIY AIR FRESHENING SPRAY

Here's a way to customize your own room spray. I prefer this to a diffuser because I do not like the idea of such a steady stream of essential oils in the air, though they can be used safely at short intervals. But I find this room spray to be just the right amount for a scent cue.

A non-scented alcohol such as vodka (isopropyl, or rubbing, alcohol is usually denatured with a bittering agent, which is not what you want here)
Water
Your favorite essential oil(s)
An empty Dr. Bronner's Hand Sanitizer bottle or any fine-misting spray bottle

For the 2-ounce Dr. Bronner's Hand Sanitizer bottle, fill the bottle halfway with the alcohol and the rest of the way with the water. For the scent, start with 10 drops of your favorite essential oil or blend of oils. Swirl the solution to blend. Different oils have different intensities, so test the concentration with a few spritzes and adjust accordingly.

Do remember that essential oils are concentrated and potent, and you should not breathe them endlessly. Use them as mood cues, perks, or pick-me-ups rather than as constants, and be sure to ventilate spaces well. Also, various groups may be sensitive to them—including children, pets, people with asthma or other sensitivities—so be mindful in using them around others.

The Low Cost of Green Cleaning

Finding out that making my own cleaners saves money was an unexpected benefit. I began this journey because I wanted to reduce the risk of dangerous chemical exposure to my kids and myself. But the fact that this all costs less? It's icing on the cake!

I bring this up here in the office because this is the financial center of my house. This is where I set our monthly budget and review actual spending. Because I've learned the versatility of cleaners and that cleaners do not need to vary from room to room, I no longer purchase a great variety of cleaners. This cuts down on clutter as well as expense.

Here I've listed my four most-used ingredients in my GIY arsenal: Dr. Bronner's Pure-Castile Liquid Soap, Dr. Bronner's Sal Suds, baking soda, and vinegar. To figure out the savings, take the purchase price for the product and divide it by the bottles of cleaning solution you get from that one product.

DR. BRONNER'S PURE-CASTILE LIQUID SOAP (32-OUNCE BOTTLE):

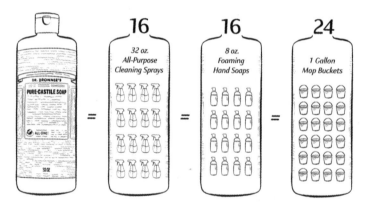

DR. BRONNER'S SAL SUDS BIODEGRADABLE CLEANER (32-OUNCE BOTTLE):

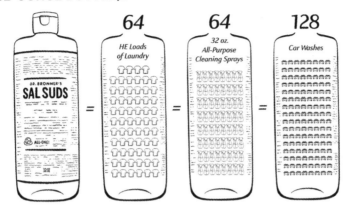

BAKING SODA (3.5-POUND BAG):

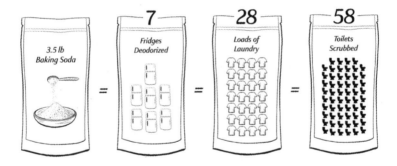

WHITE DISTILLED VINEGAR (1 GALLON; 4 L):

INGREDIENT SPOTLIGHT
Peppermint Oils

Dr. Bronner's is the largest user of organic and fair trade peppermint oil in the world. It is our signature scent and our fourth-most-used ingredient. Spicy, fresh, and utterly iconic, much of our supply comes from Pavitramenthe, an operation in the northern Indian state of Uttar Pradesh. Pavitramenthe was one of the first companies in the world to earn Regenerative Organic Certification® Silver status in 2020. Working with over 2,500 farmers on more than 10,000 acres of land, Pavitramenthe has brought key regenerative principles, such as composting, minimal soil tillage, cover cropping, and diversification to rejuvenate depleted farmlands. While they supply Dr. Bronner's with three types of mint oils—piperita, arvensis, and spicata—the farmers also produce herbs, vegetables, spices, and nitrogen-fixing legumes, such as lentils, beans, peas, and peanuts, which pull nitrogen out of the air and deposit it into in the soil, where it is a needed nutrient. This diversity not only strengthens each crop and improves the soil but also provides the farmers with financial stability from multiple income sources and year-round harvesting.

Through the fair trade fund, Pavitramenthe has been able to support menstrual hygiene advocacy, distributing washable and reusable menstrual pads and providing much-needed education to girls and families on the topic. This paves the way for girls to maintain their educational track and achieve higher goals. The fund has also provided medical camps, bathroom facilities, and clean drinking water to many sites in the region.

Ask Lisa

Q Why do electronics get dusty faster than other surfaces?

A The simple answer is electromagnetism. Every electronic device has an electromagnetic field that attracts any passing dust. This is why your touch screen gets dusty moments after you have cleaned it. Regular dusting and vacuuming in the room will help electronics stay clean longer.

Q Why do you recommend dusting with microfiber cloths when those shed microplastics in the laundry that end up in the water supply?

A This is a very real concern. I stick by microfiber cloths because they are highly absorbent and hold up to seven times their weight in moisture, and they dry very quickly. Their fibers are grippy to pick up dust and debris, they don't leave lint, and they are durable. I have had my set of microfiber cloths for over 10 years. However, microfiber does shed microplastics, particularly for the first seven washes. The solution is to use a fiber filter bag, a microfiber catching ball, or a filter attached to the discharge hose.

Q Can I use your Pure-Castile Soap as a room freshener, in an essential oil diffuser, or in a humidifier?

A No, this is not a good idea. I understand that this question is a compliment indicating that the soaps smell so good. However, if it were diffused into the air, it would eventually fall onto surfaces and coat them. Soap works by attracting dirt. A soap coating on household surfaces would become very dirty. Also, anything diffused into the air gets inhaled into our lungs. Soap is not meant to be inhaled. With humidifiers, often some sort of bacteriostatic solution is recommended in order for the appliance to stay clean. Soap does not work in this way. Please consult the user guide for a recommendation.

CHAPTER 6

THE BACKYARD

I go to nature to be soothed and healed, and to have my senses put in order.
—JOHN BURROUGHS

My relationship with the outdoors has evolved greatly in my years in the country. I've always loved the outdoors, but growing up in suburban Los Angeles, it was more of a theoretical enjoyment. Though the idea of windswept mountaintops and wildflower meadows made my heart swell, most of the outdoors I experienced were carefully controlled. Swimming pools, soccer fields, front lawns. Moving to the country gave the outdoors a whole new definition, wild and unexpected in its beauty and its offerings.

Two years into our country dwelling, we welcomed into our home a black Labrador named Tucker—the sweetest, friendliest fellow you ever would meet. He loved to bring us gifts. Every time we walked in the door, or if he just hadn't seen us in a while because we'd been in another room or he'd been napping, Tucker would greet us with a gift. Whatever was handy. He'd look around in desperation until he found something really good. Really special. A sock, a shoe, a napkin, a kid's wayward underwear. And he loved it when we made a big deal about it.

"Wow, Tuxie! A tube of toothpaste *and* a shin guard! You shouldn't have!" He knew then that we understood the depths of his affection.

He outdid himself one day. We had just arrived home with the usual hurricane of two kids and a baby pouring into the house. Tucker was thrilled to see us. He had been outside and hurried in to greet me in the nursery, where I was changing a diaper. Dangling from the side of his mouth was half a dead snake.

Tucker was ecstatic beyond all hope with the excitement he generated. Never had I shrieked with such joy over one of his gifts! He promptly dropped his gift on the nursery floor and joined me in my dance of glee.

My firstborn has always been my calm in such moments. Clearheaded and decisive, his six-year-old self assessed the situation and then ran to the kitchen and came back with a piece of plastic wrap. With it he gathered up the half snake and whisked it into the trash.

This was by no means the last time the outside came inside unexpectedly. Lizards, scorpions, black widows, birds, squirrels, mice, and whole live snakes have all found themselves, much to their consternation and mine, in our house. Most we've successfully relocated, but I do prefer when the outside stays outside. It works better when they're the host and I'm the visitor, rather than vice versa.

Despite the wildness of the outdoors, or maybe because of it, when the world is too much with me, I escape outside. There I can sync with the seasons and cycles of the year. The ebb and flow, the passing and returning of time. The rhythms surround and soothe and reposition me. I feel the journey of the wind across the land, the journey of the Earth around the sun, the rhythm of creation, the pulse of the skies.

These rhythms are lullabies to the soul, smoothing the small indignities that can loom large, reminding me there is a far bigger story going on here. It is a relief to realize that I am not at the center of the world, nor am I responsible for it, a burden I cannot bear. All that is left to me is to do what I can where I am with what I have. The rhythms of the natural world simultaneously humble me and give me strength.

There are practical ways I align with these rhythms. One is the regular morning tea time with Michael I mentioned back in the first chapter. There does come a time when it is too cold, even when I'm bundled still in my bathrobe and slippers, wrapped around my warm cup of tea, and we have to move inside. Eagerly I await the spring, when we can rejoin the harmony of the waking world, which never fails to position my day and its small challenges properly. Similarly, my family has a tradition of eating ice cream drumsticks after dinner on the front porch.

Another way I sync with the seasons is through gardening. I am an earnest, if not always successful, gardener. I start each year with great ambition, with every intention of creating an orderly and productive garden. For weeks I tend my crop daily, checking for intruders, be they plant or animal. I drape netting over the top to keep out rabbits and birds and carefully tie vines to the trellis to make sure everything has the support it needs. Everything is tidy and cared for, rows of green promise.

Then a busy life stretch comes and I miss getting out to the garden for a week or two. The next time I visit, the pumpkin vines are in bed with the peppers; the tomatoes have intertwined so thoroughly I can't tell which type is where; the pole beans have overwhelmed and toppled their supports, which now lie helplessly strangled by the advancing vines; and the zucchinis are the size of baseball bats. From then on, gardening is a free-for-all, with the plants surging out every which way while I flounder uselessly on the sidelines. Occasionally I'll attempt to assert some leadership by pruning and re-trellising, but the garden knows which one of us is in charge. So long as it gives forth a bountiful harvest, we both can be happy. It behooves us both for there to be produce, and though I have to dive through a sea of green, the garden gives forth its fecund offerings faster than I can keep up.

A third way I sync with the seasons is through a subscription to a CSA program. CSA stands for Community Supported Agriculture, a concept whose motto should be "support your local farmer." These are farm boxes filled with whatever is in season. It is a surprise, except that year after year, the cycle repeats, so I know when the strawberries in the box will give way to watermelons, which eventually will disappear in lieu of pumpkins. With a CSA box, I am getting what is most in season, which some research suggests aligns with the nutrients our bodies need most at that time of year, and I am supporting local agriculture. My food arrives more full of nutrients, not having lost any in long transit or shelf-sitting.

Although I have the advantage of a sizable yard with space and light, as well as a chest freezer and pantry to freeze and preserve the output, I encourage you to microsync with the seasons by growing at least one plant. Keep close this reminder that we are intrinsically connected to the soil, no matter how urban and artificial our lives may get. Grow something to have life near, to nurture and care for another living thing, which always results in nurturing and caring for ourselves. Grow a potted herb, a houseplant, a cactus. Grow a fruit tree in a pot on your patio and marvel at the cycle of the season occurring even here. Grow something.

GOING GREEN IN THE BACKARD

When summer peaks over the horizon and the days lengthen and the air warms, there comes a weekend in which the dormant outdoor kit must awaken from their winter slumber to prep for their season. Armed with buckets and rags and squeegees and trowels, we traipse outside to wipe down furniture, wash windows, and spruce up the hanging baskets.

For the most part, I recommend using the Sal Suds Biodegradable Cleaner instead of the Pure-Castile Soap on hardscaping, such as cement and brick, as well as on shiny surfaces like cars. Whichever one you use, it is fine for the excess to run off into grass, garden beds, and the like. They both readily biodegrade.

RECIPES AND HOW-TOS

CLEANING OUTDOOR FURNITURE

1. Add ½ tablespoon (7.5 ml) Sal Suds to a gallon of water in a bucket. Dunk in a cloth or a stiff brush and clean patio tables, chairs, lounges, cushions, and pillows. At this dilution there's no need to rinse unless you see abundant bubbles on surfaces. Dry reflective furniture to prevent water spots, particularly in hard water conditions.

2. If all you have is the Pure-Castile Soap, you can make a similar washing bucket with 2 tablespoons (30 ml) Pure-Castile Soap in a bucket of water. Wash furniture over grass or dirt to prevent white residue on bricks or concrete. After washing the furniture, dry fully with a cloth.

3. On clear glass tabletops, use the above dilution to clean off dust, dirt, and grime, then follow up with the Glass Cleaning spray. Spray and wipe with a microfiber cloth.

PRESSURE WASHING

Fill the solution chamber with water and add 1 drop of Sal Suds. Use the pressure washer as directed. Unless you see bubbles remaining on the surface, there is no need to rinse, and because it's biodegradable, the runoff won't harm plants.

WINDOW WASHING

Window washing is best done on an overcast day, or early in the morning before the windows have heated up with the light of the sun. The GIY All-Purpose Cleaning Spray will remove the grime from windows, but sometimes I find this dilution to be too strong, leaving too many suds. In that case, I make a Lite version.

1 tablespoon (15 ml) Pure-Castile Soap OR ½ teaspoon (2.5 ml) Sal Suds
1 quart (1 L) water

HOW TO:

1. Fill the spray bottle with the water and then add the soap or Suds.

2. Spray windows and wash with a wet (more than damp) cloth.

3. Squeegee. (I really think squeegee-ing works best here.)

4. If needed, follow up with a spray of GIY Glass Cleaner (page 93) and then a squeegee.

5. Wipe the window rims.

WASHING WINDOW SCREENS

To get the most impact out of washing your windows, you also need to wash the screens. Screens catch a lot of debris, and you'd be amazed at how much more light is able to come through them once they're cleaned.

HOW TO:

1. Remove your screens and lay them flat.

2. In a wash bucket, combine ½ tablespoon (7.5 ml) Sal Suds in 3 gallons (12 L) of water.

3. Wet the screens with a hose.

4. Dunk a long-handled brush or window/car scrubber in the bucket and scrub the screens.

5. Flip the screens and scrub them again.

6. Rinse well with the hose.

7. Stand the screens against a wall to air dry before reinstalling.

Other Window Washing Tips

+ Wait until the sun is not shining on windows to wash them. A cloudy day or the morning or evening is best.
+ Wipe/squeegee one side vertically and the other horizontally, so if there's a streak you'll know which side it is on.
+ Wash windows top to bottom so you can catch any drips.
+ Wipe the squeegee on a rag or towel after each pass to remove liquid and prevent drips.
+ Wipe the rims of the glass last to catch residual spray or streaks.

✦ Look at the glass from the side to see if you caught all the streaks and spots.

✦ Use a razor blade (carefully!!) to remove paint or who-knows-what on glass. Take care not to scratch the glass or cut yourself.

Car Washing

One of the first ways I ever used Sal Suds after I had launched solo into my adulthood was washing my car. I didn't own a hose, so I took advantage of a convenient downpour to run out and give the car a quick scrub with the Suds. The rain quickly rinsed it and the job was done.

CAR WASHING—EXTERIOR

1. Add ½ tablespoon (7.5 ml) Sal Suds to a bucket of water. Use a stiff brush on the wheels and a microfiber mitt on the car. Rinse well with a hose—I recommend adding a control nozzle to reduce water waste—and dry with microfiber cloths.

2. Pure club soda in a spray bottle is the best natural hack for windows, mirrors, and lights. Spray and wipe with a microfiber cloth. The club soda removes any water spots and won't harm the wax.

CAR WASHING—INTERIOR

We strap ourselves into our cars after touching public railings, shopping cart handles, gas pumps, money, other people's hands, our cell phones, and countless other reservoirs of germs and dirt. Then we touch the door handle, the seatbelt, the key, the steering wheel, the radio, the gearshift, the armrest—transferring all that whatever to every surface in our car. Further, that grime on the inside of windows is from the outgassing of the materials in your car, combined with any pollutants in the air, all blended with what you might be breathing out yourself.

All that adds up to a daunting layer of dirt and dust and grime and gore. And yet we tend to wash the outsides of our cars more than the insides.

We also keep our cars sealed up pretty tight, keeping the heat in or out depending on the time of year. This means that any fumes from cleaners are going to be kept in the car, and we are going to breathe them in repeatedly.

1. Begin by vacuuming the car thoroughly, using the wand attachment on your machine. Get all the dirt and crumbs out of the crevices of the seat cushions. Remove the floor mats and vacuum them flat on the driveway. If the upholstery needs cleaning, spot-clean with the GIY All-Purpose Cleaning Spray (page 91), or for larger sections or the carpeting, use a carpet cleaner (see The Family Room) with the upholstery attachment.

2. Clean the dashboard, steering wheel, doors, handles, center console, cup holders, and other surfaces with the GIY All-Purpose Cleaning Spray and a damp cloth. Do not spray electronics directly, but rather spray the cloth and then wipe the electronics.

3. For the windows and mirrors, if they are particularly grimy, spray with the GIY All-Purpose Cleaning Spray and wipe with a damp cloth. If they are only lightly dirty, spray with GIY Glass Cleaner (page 93), and wipe with a dry cloth. Be sure you clean windows thoroughly, or the next glare of sunlight will reveal missed swipes.

4. In lieu of air fresheners, which contain all the hazards of fragrance in concentration, spritz the air with Dr. Bronner's Peppermint or Lavender Hand Sanitizer.

SOAP AS GARDEN SPRAY

The USDA's NOP lists insecticidal soap as an allowed pest control measure for organic crops. Soap must be wet when it contacts pests to be effective. The residue is not effective.

1 tablespoon (15 ml) Dr. Bronner's Pure-Castile Soap
1 quart (1 L) water

1. Combine the soap and water in a spray bottle.

2. Spray plants thoroughly. Be sure to spray stems and under the leaves, where bugs hide. Spray early in the morning or evening so that the heat of the day does not evaporate the spray immediately and it is effective longer. You may need to spray plants daily for a while to thwart an intense infestation.

NOTE: All scents are equally effective, although I recommend a food-ish scent, just in case the plants absorb some of the essential oils. Peppermint, Citrus, and Unscented are all great options. If your water is particularly hard, consider using distilled or filtered water so mineral deposits don't build up on leaves.

Although my research indicated a soap spray will not harm beneficial insects like bees and ladybugs, you can be sure not to bother any by giving the plant a quick shake before spraying.

HOW TO USE HAND SANITIZER

Not only is there a proper way to use hand sanitizer, there is a proper place to use hand sanitizer. Do not use hand sanitizer if soap and water are available, because soap and water are more effective ways to rid hands of germs. This is why I bring it up here in the outdoors. Other places hand sanitizer is the best option are when traveling, running errands, or eating a snack on the go. In order for hand sanitizer to be most effective, there are a few steps to remember:

1. Coat the surfaces of your hands with sanitizer, including your palms, the backs of your hands, and your fingertips.

2. Rub your hands thoroughly until dry.

3. Do not wipe off wet hand sanitizer. It needs to stay on your hands until it evaporates to do its job. Keep rubbing your hands until dry.

What to Look for in a Hand Sanitizer

✦ Read the ingredients. For so many reasons, read the ingredients. Look for an active ingredient of ethyl alcohol over 60 percent or isopropyl alcohol over 70 percent.

  Avoid "alcohol-free." This could indicate that the active ingredient is benzalkonium chloride, which is less effective than alcohol.

  Ignore "FDA-approved." This is a marketing gimmick. All hand sanitizers must be registered with the FDA, but the FDA does not authorize the use of this statement.

  Avoid artificial fragrances and other synthetic additives.

Off-Label Uses for Hand Sanitizer

I always have this with me when I am out and about and end up using it for so many uses beyond hand cleaning.

  Deodorant in a pinch. (Most malodors are caused by bacteria. Kill the bacteria and you reduce the odors.)

  Body-refreshing mist. (The Peppermint on a hot day is especially cooling!)

  Stickiness eliminator.

✦ Deodorizing shoe spray.

✦ Air freshener.

  Cat deterrent for chewing indoor plants. Spritz the tips of plants lightly with the hand sanitizer to give them a bitter taste that will deter nibbling cats.

Sunscreen

If you're looking for a safe way to sunbathe and get a good tan, there isn't one. After a small bout with skin cancer on my forehead, I have realized the necessity of daily sunscreen, not just on days where "being outside" is a major activity.

To give you a quick summary of what I buy: I look for mineral-based sunscreens (zinc oxide and titanium dioxide), SPF 35–50, with few total ingredients, no retinyl palmitate, no parabens, and no fragrance. If I do for some reason need to buy a chemical sunscreen, I look for ones without oxybenzone and octinoxate.

The best sun protection involves a multifaceted approach and does not depend on sunscreen alone. Include in your sun protection attentiveness to timing, clothing, and shade.

TIMING: Avoid the midday sun—between 10 a.m. and 1 p.m.

CLOTHING: Wear a hat, long sleeves and pants, or cover-up when possible in the sun. Opt for fabrics with a UPF of 30 or higher. In lieu of that, choose loose-fitting, dark, or brightly colored clothing in a densely woven fabric.

SHADE: Use an umbrella at the beach or poolside or a shade tree at the park.

Tips for Choosing and Using Sunscreen

BROAD SPECTRUM: Choose a sunscreen with broad spectrum coverage, meaning it blocks both UVA and UVB rays.

APPLICATION: Apply sunscreen 20 to 30 minutes before sun exposure and reapply frequently throughout the day and after swimming and sweating. Use 1 ounce of sunscreen at each application for the whole body. One ounce is 2 tablespoons, enough to fill an adult's hand. It might be the whole tube of travel-sized sunscreen. Yes, that's a lot. This is how it is intended to be applied, and any promise of protection is for this amount of application.

READ INGREDIENTS EVERY TIME YOU BUY: This frustrates me every year! Many sunscreen manufacturers change formulations from year to year. Even within the same line, ingredients can be completely different from one product to another. Kids SPF 50 Sport and Kids SPF 50 Waterproof may not have any active ingredients in common. Read all ingredients for every bottle each time you stock up. I wish I could make it easier.

Other Sunscreen Factors to Question

DON'T ASK TOO MUCH OF YOUR SUNSCREEN: It's better to have one product that does one thing well (blocking the sun) rather than doing two or more things—whether it's antiaging, self-tanning, wrinkle smoothing, bug repelling, or makeup foundation—less than well.

SPF OVER 60: Studies have not shown increased efficacy in SPFs marked over 60, which can give a false sense of security and be a marketing gimmick.

RETINYL PALMITATE (VITAMIN A): This is an inactive ingredient often touted as giving antiaging benefits to a product, but in the presence of sunlight it encourages tumor growth. Avoid it in sunscreens.

SPRAY AND POWDER SUNSCREENS: These pose an inhalation risk. They give convenience but trade the risk of ingredients being absorbed through the lungs that aren't easily absorbed through the skin. If you do use a spray, spray it outside.

"ORGANIC" SUNSCREEN: None of the active sunscreen ingredients can be organic—they're either mineral or chemical. Perhaps some of the inactive ingredients are organic, but make sure it's not a gimmick.

"WATERPROOF," "SWEATPROOF," "TOWELPROOF": These terms are proving to be false. All sunscreens are diminished by swimming, sweating, or toweling off. Sunscreen needs to be reapplied after swimming, after sweating, and/or every 2 hours.

"CHEMICAL-FREE": I haven't a clue what this term means. Perhaps it means "toxic chemical–free" or that the active ingredients are minerals (zinc and titanium). Still, read the ingredient list to find out.

"REEF SAFE": Meant to indicate ingredients don't harm delicate coral reefs, but there is no agreed-upon definition. Because this term isn't strictly regulated, sunscreen manufacturers aren't required to test and demonstrate that such products won't harm aquatic life. Mineral sunscreens pose less risk than chemical sunscreens.

And if this is all just a little overwhelming, the simplest statement to keep in mind is that wearing any sunscreen is better than not wearing sunscreen.

Clean Camping with Dr. Bronner's

During the summers I worked in my grandfather's office, I became familiar with some of the stores that bought the products. Certain names would snag in my memory, though I knew nothing about them. Then, in my sojourn in North Carolina, during one of many beautiful treks up into the Great Smoky Mountains, we found ourselves at the Nantahala Outdoor Center. Immediately, my grandfather's files sprang to mind, and I recalled that they had been buying the soap for decades. It was like meeting an old friend for the first time.

Many people first encounter our soaps while camping. That is because its versatility and biodegradability make it the ideal trail companion. The National Parks recommend a biodegradable soap when camping, and many camping outlets specify Dr. Bronner's. Outdoor etiquette mandates washing 200 feet from any water source and using a bottle of water. Here are some ways to keep clean and healthy when next you head out for some time under the stars.

Ways Dr. Bronner's keeps your body clean while camping:

+ Dr. Bronner's Pure-Castile Liquid Soap for washing hands, face, body, hair, even teeth (yes, it tastes like soap!).
+ Dr. Bronner's All-One Toothpaste (if you don't want to use the Pure-Castile Soap).
+ Dr. Bronner's Organic Hand Sanitizer for after bathroom breaks and before cooking and eating if soap and water are not an option.

✦ Baby Unscented GIY Baby Wipes (page 69) or when running water isn't available, wash up with Wipe-Off Castile Body Wash Spray (page 46).

Ways Dr. Bronner's keeps your stuff clean while camping:

DISHES: Set up two tubs of water. Squirt some Pure-Castile Soap or Sal Suds into the first tub. Wash dishes and rinse in the second tub. If drains are not available, be sure to pour out the water 200 feet from a water source and not near your campsite, where the food smells might attract wildlife.

CLOTHES: Place clothes in a sealable plastic bag or closed container. Add water and a squirt of soap. Agitate the container, or if it's a day of travel, leave the containers to jostle about in the back of your vehicle. At the end of the day, rinse out the clothes and hang to dry. This is how John Steinbeck did it in *Travels with Charley*. I like to think that he might have used my grandfather's soap. It was 1962, and he had roots in California, so it is possible!

TENTS AND OTHER GEAR: Should you need to wash your tent—say, you pitched it under a shady pine tree and it's now dappled with sap—dilute a squirt of the Pure-Castile Soap or Sal Suds in a cup of water and spot clean with a washcloth. Rinse with a clean wet washcloth. The most important part of keeping your tent and other textile gear in tip-top shape is making sure it is dry before you put it away.

Whenever you're in the outdoors, backpacking, camping, hiking, or at a park, remember more wise words from my mom and Scouts everywhere: leave the place better than you found it. My own definition of green.

GIY FIRE STARTER

My favorite part of camping is sitting around a crackling fire, telling stories, making s'mores, or simply staring into its depths. I know that fire building is a skill that some people take great pride in. I am not a great fire builder, but I can get one going, especially if I have one of these handy fire starters. A reader first gave me this idea, and I thought it was brilliant. I played around with it for a bit and came up with this version.

> Cotton dryer lint—make sure it's cotton. Collect the lint after
> drying a load of fluffy cotton towels or flannel sheets. You can
> also use cotton pads or balls.
>
> Dr. Bronner's Virgin Coconut Oil, liquified
>
> Beeswax, liquified in a double boiler

HOW TO:

1. Roll cotton dryer lint into balls.

2. Using a long fork (mine was a fondue stick), dip the balls in liquid coconut oil until saturated. Place on a piece of parchment paper on a plate. Refrigerate the balls 5 to 10 minutes, or until the coconut oil hardens.

3. Again, using the long fork, dip the balls into the liquid beeswax until they are completely coated. Refrigerate another 10 minutes until the beeswax hardens. Store at room temperature.

4. To use, break open a fire starter so the lint is exposed and place it on the grate with kindling arranged over it. Light the lint. Mine burn for 15 to 20 minutes, plenty of time to get the kindling going, and then I lay the larger logs on top of the flames.

ANIMAL WASHING

As far as animals go, I have only ever owned dogs and cats and have only ever washed dogs and cats, the latter most reluctantly for both of us. However, I have heard so many wonderful stories over the years about all manner of animals enjoying their baths with Pure-Castile Soap: horses, sheep, chickens and other birds, pigs.

The simplicity that makes the Pure-Castile Soap great for our bodies also makes it great for animals. No junk. No fillers. No irritants or cloying artificial fragrances. Plus, soaps like the Pure-Castile are on the NOP list of approved insecticides and so, although it won't give residual protection, it does clean them off beautifully. If dealing with a flea infestation, be sure to also launder your pet's bed and bedding frequently with either the Pure-Castile Soap or Sal Suds and high heat.

Whether or not to predilute the soap here depends on the animal's coat and your preference. If the animal's coat will hold a tremendous amount of water, I would not predilute the soap. The water held in the fur or feathers will dilute the soap effectively. However, if the animal has a thin coat that does not hold much water, prediluting may help spread the soap more easily. For example, the aforementioned Tucker had an extremely thick coat that held a ton of water. I did not predilute the soap with him. My other pooch, Sadie, has a much thinner coat—so much so that she enjoys getting tucked in each night with a blanket—and so I find it easier to use a prediluted solution on her. For her, I take a cup of water and add 1 tablespoon (15 ml) of soap in the cup.

There are concerns about using essential oils on animals. These concerns mostly revolve around using undiluted essential oils on their skin or regularly diffusing essential oils into the air that they breathe. With Dr. Bronner's Pure-Castile Soaps, not only are the essential oils present at no more than a 2 percent concentration, but soap is also a wash-off product, so the exposure time is minimal. However, if this is a concern for you, use the Baby Unscented Pure-Castile Soap. For cats, who are particularly sensitive to essential oils, stick with the Unscented.

My dad taught me the blend he called "Euco Peppo Bear Wash"—made of equal amounts Eucalyptus and Peppermint Pure-Castile Soap—which is what he used on our dogs. It's a tingly, woodsy combo. If you'd like something subtler, the Lavender makes for a soothing scent for animals and owners alike.

HOW TO:

To wash, wet the animal thoroughly. Apply soap—straight or diluted. Massage all over, avoiding ears and eyes. (As I've covered, soap is not tear-free.) Rinse the animal thoroughly. Dry well.

The Sal Suds and Pure-Castile Soap are also super handy for washing bedding, feeding gear, leashes, collars, carriers, and toys. They keep everything in great shape with no residues to harm or deter.

GIY NO-CHEW SPRAY

I had need of this spray when we got our most recent rescue, Sadie. She is a Heinz-57 mutt who styles herself adorably with one ear up, one ear down. Cute as she is, we don't much fancy her chewing on shoes and furniture. I continued to use this with our pair of bonded cats, the female of which loves chewing on windowsills, chair arms, bookshelves. Her brother loves chewing on plants. A quick spritz of this spray redirects their chewing to more agreed-upon objects.

⅓ **cup (80 ml) apple cider vinegar**
⅔ **cup (160 ml) regular white vinegar**

HOW TO:

1. Combine in a small spray bottle. An empty Dr. Bronner's Hand Sanitizer bottle works great for this.

2. Spot-test this spray discreetly on a surface before use. Spritz the surface lightly to deter chewing.

LAB COAT MOMENT
Impact of Essential Oils

While the primary purpose of the essential oils is to scent each of the Pure-Castile Liquid Soaps, they also impact the soaps in other ways. For one, they change the color of the soaps slightly, and for another, they change the freezing point of the soap.

You can observe this by pouring ½ cup (120 ml) of varying scents of the Pure-Castile into different clear jars or glasses. Place the jars in the fridge or outside on a cold day. Check on them every 5 minutes and observe when they begin to turn white. This is a sign that they are starting to "freeze," or turn solid, even though it is a far higher temperature than the freezing point of water. Insert an instant-read thermometer into each scent to note the exact temperature at which it becomes white. Label the jar with this temperature and the corresponding scent.

While it is not a drastic difference from one scent to the next, the slight difference is a guide. If you were to leave these jars outside, you could judge the day's temperature, within a certain range, based on the varying clarity of the soap. Or you could leave the soaps at room temperature where they will return to their original clear amber hue and be ready for your next washing need.

Ask Lisa

Q Why do Dr. Bronner's Pure-Castile Soaps and Sal Suds Biodegradable Cleaner turn white?

A Cold temperatures will cause both of these products to turn white. Usually this happens when they are stored in a garage or shed or perhaps taken camping. There is absolutely nothing wrong with the product. If the soap is still semiliquid, go ahead and use it. If it has solidified, bring it into a warm room for a day, or if you're in a hurry, place it in a bowl or sink of warm water. The soap will reliquify and clarify. This does not impact its quality. (I must say: do not microwave, bake, or heat the soap on a stove.)

That it does this is a sign of its purity. Pure virgin coconut oil, a key ingredient in these products, has a freezing point of 76°F (24.5°C). While the other ingredients in the products lower this point, you will still find that they both turn cloudy and then white as the temperature approaches 60°F (16°C).

Q Can I use your soaps to wash glasses and sunglasses?

A Yes, both the Pure-Castile Soap and the Sal Suds are great options for any sort of eyeglasses. They are mild cleansers that will not affect the coatings on the glasses. You can clean them with a drop of pure soap or Sal Suds or with a dollop from a foaming pump dispenser or with a spray of GIY All-Purpose Cleaning Spray (page 91). Whichever way you choose, rub the glasses with your fingers to clean, rinse with water, and then dry them with a soft, lint-free cloth.

Q Is the soap safe in gray water and septic systems?

A This one I can speak to from personal experience as well as analyses we've had done on both the Pure-Castile Soap and the Sal Suds. I've been living with a septic system for nearly two decades now, and we've used both products for years with no issue. The products readily biodegrade and will not harm septic systems. While our soaps are made from vegetable oils, the oils are "saponified"—that is, they are turned into soaps. Our initial analysis was done specifically for their use in gray water systems in Australia, and the issues are the same for septic. The biodegradability tests show that they meet stringent criteria. When subject to water, oxygen, and microbes (all components of a septic system), they will rapidly and completely biodegrade into innocuous material that can be handled by a septic system.

Q **Does Sal Suds remove car wax?**

A The answer to this is in the ingredients, and while we all can know the ingredients in Sal Suds (clearly on the label), I have been having a very tough time finding the ingredients in specialized car wash soaps. They often say things like "mild surfactants" or "pH balanced," but that tells us absolutely nothing. It's kind of insulting, really. While it behooves manufacturers to say, "Don't use other products! Only use ours!" they're hardly unbiased and they don't provide sound reasons why, except by labeling other types of products as "harsh." Sal Suds is not harsh. I can point to my experience that Sal Suds hasn't stripped the wax off my cars, and this has been verified by in-house testing. It does not, however, contain any waxing ingredients or any residual protectants.

CHAPTER 7

THE FAMILY ROOM

People forget facts, but they remember stories.
—JOSEPH CAMPBELL

The maxim says the family that prays together stays together, but there's also something deeply bonding for the family that reads together.

Michael and I have read books aloud to our kids after dinner for years. We start at the table and transition to the sofa. It started when the kids were little, and in my effort to instill good table manners, I decreed that everyone would stay seated at the table until everyone was finished.

I shot myself in the foot with that one.

My husband was in grad school at night, so it was often just me and the kids. I soon realized I birthed the world's slowest eaters, and I was battling boredom and impatience. To save my own sanity and preserve the lesson, I began reading to them while they finished. We still do this today, even as they are old enough to vote.

Some books have been silly and joyful, others more serious. *Rascal* by Sterling North. *Cheaper by the Dozen* by the Gilbreths. *At Home in Mitford* by Jan Karon. Steinbeck's *Travels with Charley* and *The Short Reign of Pippin IV*.

Sharing the experience and the emotion of reading together has brought us closer and has sparked many conversations. Whenever our lives are disparate and difficult and out of sync, we travel together through the pages of a book.

I had no TV growing up. The story goes that one day when we were preschoolers, the TV broke. My dad, heading out to work, muttered, "Oh, just get rid of it." So by the time he got back home, it was gone. Instead of television, I grew up on books and radio. To this day I find watching baseball uninspiring, compared to the soothing and captivating voice of Vin Scully, who wove every Dodgers game into an epic tale. Evenings were spent sprawled across our family room, reading or playing games.

All this to say, stories have saturated my life. My dad was a master storyteller. I don't know who enjoyed Pop's stories more, him or his audience. His eyes, wide and blue, would stare into the distance, seeing events unfold in his mind's eye as he narrated them to us. He would pause and chuckle and lean forward in such a way that held us spellbound.

He had plenty of occasion to tell his stories because not infrequently he would take us to some restaurant he'd heard tell of and they often had really long waits. My dad had two ways of dealing with impatient kids: playing 20 Questions and telling us stories. We loved both. We would ask repeatedly for our favorite stories, awaiting the punchlines we knew by heart.

"Tell the one about the pennies in the bar!" "The motorcycle on the dock!" "The toilet on the car!" "The fire in the boiler room!" Most of his stories stemmed from his Navy days, likely tamed for our young ears.

One of my favorites evidenced the perfect combination of my dad's professional capability and private wit. I so admire his confidence and his humor in the face of pressure. He once was commissioned to create an ammunition paint for military use that could indicate whose bullets hit the targets during practice exercises. My dad soon had the product ready and called his military contact, who said they'd need to see the research he used in the development.

As you might imagine, my dad, while unparalleled at the creative and problem-solving side of inventing, was less so about the research side of anything. He'd rather find out by doing than by reading and demonstrate rather than describe.

Undaunted, he leaned back in his chair and gazed up at a nearby shelf. His eyes rested upon the 20 Los Angeles County phonebooks—each 3 inches thick—now bullet-riddled.

"Oh yes, I have thousands of pages of research."

My dad was not officially president of Dr. Bronner's very long, from 1994 until 1998, but the role he played was crucial to its survival. Most family businesses do not survive the transition from the founder to the next generation. My parents, alongside my Uncle Ralph, carefully made this happen. My dad's presidency connected the 45-plus years my grandfather ran the organization to the 25 years and counting of my brothers' tenure.

In 2015, the company articulated six Cosmic Principles to describe and guide our business relationships and decisions. In them, I hear my parents' voices and see evidence of the tenets by which they ran the household where I grew up.

"Do your best and don't give up" became
+ **Cosmic Principle #1: Work Hard! Grow!**
"Be honest and authentic with people" became
+ **Cosmic Principle #2: Do right by customers.**
"Our door is always open and everyone has a place at our table" became
+ **Cosmic Principle #3: Treat employees like family.**
"Don't take advantage of people" became
+ **Cosmic Principle #4: Be fair to suppliers.**
"Leave the place better than you found it" became
+ **Cosmic Principle #5: Treat the earth like home.**
"Do what you can where you are" became
+ **Cosmic Principle #6: Fund and fight for what's right.**

Even while there is so much of my grandfather, the company headquarters strongly recalls my childhood home and my parents' principles for living. I see it in these guiding principles and in more tangible tributes, from the practical to the fun. After all, my dad's Snofoam became our Magic Foam Experience, which brings the joy of a foam shower blasted high in the air, to company gatherings, children's centers, and community festivals.

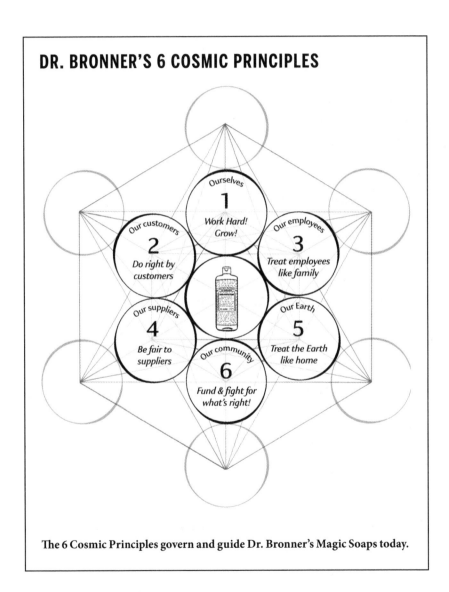

DR. BRONNER'S 6 COSMIC PRINCIPLES

Ourselves
1
Work Hard! Grow!

Our customers
2
Do right by customers

Our employees
3
Treat employees like family

Our suppliers
4
Be fair to suppliers

Our Earth
5
Treat the Earth like home

Our community
6
Fund & fight for what's right!

The 6 Cosmic Principles govern and guide Dr. Bronner's Magic Soaps today.

GOING GREEN IN THE FAMILY ROOM

The Family Room is a place to let our guards down. This is a place where we turn off, where we can relax. Growing up, what I'd call a family room now we called a den. Probably because it was half-underground, courtesy of the hill my house was built on. It was really dark, especially with the hammered green glass French doors that were the height of fashion. This was where my dad suspended that roast from the ceiling and where I learned to play Hearts and where, in my adolescence, we did once again put a TV in order to watch the underdog Los Angeles Dodgers beat the Oakland A's in the 1988 World Series, spurred by one of the greatest moments in sports history: the epic walk-off homerun in Game 1 by the injured Kirk Gibson.

RECIPES AND HOW-TOS

DUSTING

Regular dusting is critical to a hygienic home. Even the dust you cannot see is important to wipe up because it breeds all manner of mites and harbors pollutants and toxins. Dusting is far simpler than any product advertising you will see. No extra input is needed other than water on a soft, absorbent, lint-free cloth. Various dusting sprays do not collect dust better than a damp cloth and can build up residues on your surfaces. So my instructions for dusting are super simple: dust often with a soft, damp cloth.

CLEANING CARPETS

Floors are the largest horizontal surface in our living spaces. They need your attention. If you need the place to look cleaner fast, tend to the floors. If you don't have time for a full-on carpet cleaning, at least give them a thorough vacuuming. It makes a big impact.

Vacuum carpets regularly and thoroughly. This extends the life of the carpets and suppresses dust and allergens. Vacuums with HEPA filters keep fine particles out of the air.

I keep my carpets in order with spot cleaning, but for a deeper cleaning, I bring out my carpet cleaning machine. I used to rent these, but then had so much occasion to use them—sigh—that it was more economical to own one.

Both Sal Suds and Pure-Castile Soap are great on carpets. Not only do they work great, but they don't leave fragrance residues—or any residues—that could be harmful to pets or children. I usually opt for Sal Suds because it is slightly better at stain fighting, but the Pure-Castile Soap also works really well. I've used both over the years.

Spot-test your carpets before trying any of this by spraying an inconspicuous spot with one spray of GIY All-Purpose Cleaning Spray and rubbing vigorously with a white cloth. If there is any dye transfer, use another option on your carpets.

SPOT-CLEANING CARPETS WITH THE GIY ALL-PURPOSE CLEANING SPRAY

HOW TO:

1. If a spilled liquid has soaked in, use a highly absorbent cloth. Microfiber works particularly well. Lay it over the spot and press on it with your shoe to draw the liquid up. If the cloth becomes saturated, use a new one and repeat until no more liquid comes out.

2. Spray the spot sparingly with the GIY All-Purpose Cleaning Spray (page 91). Do not saturate the carpet with the spray, or you'll have too many bubbles in the spot. Alternatively, if it would make you feel better to spray more, then make a Lite GIY All-Purpose Cleaning Spray by using half as much soap or Sal Suds in the ratio.

3. After spraying, rub the spot with a wet (just short of drippy) rough cloth. Rub in multiple directions to scrub all sides of the carpet fibers. If that washcloth gets too soiled, get a clean one.

4. Rinse the area by using another wet cloth until all the soil and cleaner are gone.

5. Allow to dry and then vacuum to restore the texture to the area.

CLEANING WHOLE CARPETS WITH A CARPET CLEANER

HOW TO:

1. Vacuum carpets thoroughly and spot clean following the previous directions.

2. Fill the main rinsing compartment of the carpet cleaner with hot water. The heat can help loosen any grime in the carpets.

3. Fill the cleaning solution compartment with water and add either 1 drop of Sal Suds (yes, 1 drop) or ½ tablespoon (7.5 ml) Pure-Castile Soap. If your carpet cleaner has a different compartment configuration, you may have to adapt these instructions.

4. Run the carpet cleaner over the carpet according to manufacturer instructions. Take care not to oversaturate the carpet with the cleaning solution.

5. When finished, rub your fingers into the carpet to check for remaining bubbles. If you find remaining bubbles, go over again with clean water. If the rinse water looks dirty, go over the carpet again with clean water until the rinse water looks fairly clean.

NOTE: I also need to mention that using Sal Suds or Pure-Castile Soap in your carpet cleaner may void your warranty. Mind you, I'm not saying that either of these cleaners will break your machine. However, it's oftentimes a little footnote in the warranty that if you don't buy that company's brand of solution, they won't honor the warranty. You'll need to make your choice with this one. You can see that I've already made mine.

DEODORIZING CARPETS

WITH BAKING SODA

For a quick carpet freshening and deodorizing, baking soda is my go-to. It's always good to spot-test a new cleaning technique before embarking on the whole floor to make sure your carpet and your vacuum work well with baking soda. For a scented treatment, in a bowl mix 2 cups (480 ml) of baking soda with about 20 drops of a favorite essential oil. Sweet orange is always a favorite of mine. You could try lavender or something woodsy like eucalyptus. Use a fork to blend the mixture until no lumps remain. If you are sensitive to fragrance or have pets that might be, forego the essential oils. The baking soda is what's doing the work here.

HOW TO:

1. Add the baking soda to a big shaker jar. A repurposed large spice jar or a mason jar with holes in the lid work well for this.

2. Sweep the carpet with a broom to brush the powder down into the fibers.

3. Let it sit for 10 minutes.

4. Vacuum the carpet thoroughly, using a vacuum with a HEPA filter.

WITH VINEGAR

Vinegar is a more intense and more time-consuming option, but it is a great way to deodorize and lightly clean carpets. This uses the carpet cleaner again.

HOW TO:

1. Fill the main compartment with hot water plus 2 cups (480 ml) distilled white vinegar. If you would like, you can add a few drops of essential oil to the vinegar solution, or leave it as is.

2. Leave the cleaning solution compartment empty, or if the machine doesn't like it empty, just fill it with water.

3. Go over the carpets with the vinegar solution and allow to air dry.

CLEANING UPHOLSTERY

Upholstery is another place where dust likes to hide. Vacuum upholstery thoroughly and regularly, even lifting cushions and vacuuming the backs of sofas and upholstered chairs. When it comes to a deeper cleaning of spots, always test solutions in an inconspicuous area ahead of time.

For spot-cleaning, use the GIY All-Purpose Cleaning Spray. Spray the spot lightly and wipe with a wet, not drippy, cloth. Be careful in your scrubbing not to damage or remove the texture of the upholstery. Rub your finger over the spot to check for bubbles and make sure all cleaner is removed. If there are still bubbles, go over the spot again with a wet cloth. Allow to air dry. Depending on the material, you may need to fluff to restore the texture.

For whole furniture cleaning, use the upholstery attachment on the carpet cleaner and the dilution mentioned with carpets. As always, test beforehand and rinse fully afterward.

CLEANING CAT AND DOG MESSES ON CARPET

Here's an example of something from the haphazard hubbub of my house that I never anticipated discussing publicly: the variety of messes that come from one end of my animals or the other, and how to clean them up. But if you're in that situation, I know you need to know. And I have lots of experience. Sigh.

SOLID(ISH) PET MESSES

1. Pick up and dispose of any solid matter. If there is any thick liquid, try to lift this with a stiff scraper sort of tool. Anything you can lift out

of the carpet before it has a chance to sink into the fibers will make cleaning it much easier.

2. Follow carpet spot cleaning instructions on page 211.

CAT URINE

1. The chemistry of cat urine makes it require particular cleaning tactics. It's always best if you have the chance to tackle cat urine when it's fresh. (Yet another sentence I never thought I'd write.) Put dry absorbent cloths over the spot and stand on them (while wearing shoes, of course) to extract as much liquid out of the carpet as possible. Keep using fresh dry cloths until no more can be extracted.

2. Fresh cat stains contain uric acid. Neutralize this by sprinkling with baking soda. (It'll fizz.) Then spray with the GIY All-Purpose Cleaning Spray (page 91) and rub vigorously with a wet (not drippy) cloth in all directions to wash all of the carpet fibers. "Rinse" with additional wet cloths until the suds are gone. Press with dry cloths to extract all moisture. Once the area is fully dry, vacuum to remove any remaining baking soda.

3. Old cat urine stains take a different method because, as cat urine ages, its chemistry changes. It loses its acidity and develops more ammonia, which is alkaline. This is also when it begins to smell and turn yellow or gray. Spray the stain thoroughly with a half vinegar/half water spray. (It's always a good idea to spot-test this in an inconspicuous spot of carpet to test for discoloration, and yes, this is my GIY Glass Cleaner, page 93). Let this sit for 10 minutes and then rub with a wet cloth to rinse it out. Then spray lightly with the GIY All-Purpose Cleaning Spray, rub vigorously again, and follow with a clean wet cloth to rinse as above. Dry by pressing with a dry absorbent cloth. Any remaining discoloration can be treated by spraying with hydrogen peroxide (standard pharmacy grade of 3 percent). Be sure to spot-test the hydrogen peroxide first, as it can

bleach certain carpets. Work the hydrogen peroxide down into the fibers and let it sit on the stain until dry.

CLEANING WOOD FURNITURE

It is common to do too much when cleaning wood. Like so much of cleaning, don't overthink it. Don't think you have to do a lot to do a good job. Much of our current interior wood furniture is covered in surface finishes that sit on top of the wood. You're not functionally cleaning wood—you're cleaning a lacquer or varnish or polyurethane. Outdoor furniture, or even some indoor, may be finished with a penetrating finish like linseed or tung oil that needs to be reapplied. Both of the above finishes can be cleaned with soap and water. However, certain handmade or antique pieces may be finished in wax, which I find to be the trickiest of all—see special notes below.

When cleaning wood, start with the least intense cleaning method, which is dusting with a damp, soft cloth. A good microfiber cloth can remove light fingerprints with water alone. Dry the wood thoroughly after wiping. Evaluate if this is all your furniture needs. Doing more when it is not necessary upsets that risk/benefit balance I've mentioned.

If you need to take things up a notch, the GIY All-Purpose Cleaning Spray is a mild soapy solution that works great on wood. Spray the surface and wipe with a damp cloth. Be sure to dry the surface well afterward. The bane of wood is standing water.

If you think your wood may be coated in wax—more likely with an antique or handmade piece and unlikely with commercially bought wood furniture—neither water nor soap are good cleaning options. You need to look into a specialty solution for waxed furniture. Please consult your local woodworking shop.

CLEANING TRUMPETS

Without conducting a survey, I will hazard a guess that most of you do not play the trumpet or live with a trumpet player. I share this particular cleaning scenario as an example of how to clean odd things.

Because I know absolutely nothing about trumpets—playing them or cleaning them—when my oldest began playing trumpet at the age of 11, he was on his own. I gave moral support. When it came to caring for his instrument, he found tutorials that instructed him how to clean it using "a mild soap or detergent." Well, I could certainly help him with that part. Both the Pure-Castile and Sal Suds fit the bill. He opted to use the Sal Suds.

With his special set of brushes, he carefully scrubbed his instrument with the sudsy Sal Suds and threaded the tools through the tubes to clean it from the inside out. He took care not to get the wrong parts wet and afterwards dried it all with soft microfiber cloths. The trumpet was bright and shiny to play another day.

Whatever odd object you have to clean, if a mild soap or detergent is called for, that means the Pure-Castile Soap or Sal Suds.

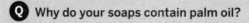

Ask Lisa

Q Why do your soaps contain palm oil?

A Palm oil is incredibly versatile, used widely in food, body care, and biofuels. It comes from an oil palm tree native to western Africa but has been transplanted worldwide in tropical regions. Because of its versatility, palm is the most common vegetable oil in the world. It is also a very dense crop, producing more oil per hectare than any other type of plant oil. Saponified in bar soaps, it produces a smooth, creamy lather that is gentle on the skin.

There has been grievous injury done to this planet, its animals, and its people for the sake of palm oil production: deforestation, habitat loss for endangered species, and gross land mismanagement. The response to these disasters has been to label palm oil as an evil crop. This fails to address the true problem. If we shun palm oil, as I've heard many vow to do, then another crop will rise to take its place, managed through the same exploitive practices. We need to target the source of the problem: the production practices.

This is exactly what Serendipalm, our sister company in Ghana that supplies us with palm oil, has successfully done. In Ghana, where oil palms are native, Dr. Bronner's has flouted naysayers and found a gorgeous way to produce palm oil involving dynamic agroforestry and regenerative organic agriculture, intercropping, biodiversity, reforestation (did you read that right? RE-forestation!), habitat restoration, soil revitalization, and carbon sequestration.

This is seriously exciting stuff. Our production of palm oil in this region is building it back up to a land bursting with nutrients and organic content, also called biomass. It is healing farms and communities by bringing them financial security and enduring land health. It is not a compromise to use palm oil. It is a benefit. Join us in encouraging other users of palm oil to demand truly ethical palm oil. As we have shown, it is more than possible.

Q Are the essential oils safe to use around my pets?

A It is good to recognize that essential oils are potent and varied compounds. Because of their surging popularity in recent years, there has been justified concern about their concentrated and indiscriminate use. When it comes to pets, concentrated exposure to essential oils is harmful because their systems cannot filter this input well. Therefore, applying undiluted or lightly diluted essential oils to their skin is not a good idea. Furthermore, diffusing essential oils into rooms they regularly occupy can be harmful.

However, using essential oils at great dilutions in cleaning solutions that are then wiped or vacuumed off of surfaces poses little risk. Nonetheless, if the idea of essential oils around pets does not sit well with you, opt for an unscented cleaner.

AFTERWORD

It is always sunrise somewhere.
—JOHN MUIR

There's an unexpected bliss to being up in the watch of the night. I would never intend to. I would never set an alarm for 2 a.m. unless there were a meteor shower. But when I awake then, after the first cycle of sleep, unable to settle into the next, I don't entirely mind getting up for a while. I only mind it because of how I might drag the next day. But as far as the moment goes, it's strangely sweet.

The house is quiet in a way it is never quiet during the day. Not just quiet but still. At rest. There is peace. A cessation of the striving that is my constant daytime companion. I have a particular love for my house at this time. I don't look around and see tasks. I look around and see home.

At these times, I go to our living room, a smaller space separate from the family room. I settle into a chair under a lamp, cat beside me, tea in hand, book open. No next thing in mind. No time crunch looming. Just now. Here.

I didn't include the living room in the preceding chapters because it is not a place of activity and its cleaning needs are similar to the family room: upholstered furniture, wood, a rug.

For years, our living room was an unused room. You could have cut it out of our house and we wouldn't have missed it. We were too busy for this place of stillness.

We need stillness and rest like masterworks of art need blank space around them. When art is well hung with blank space surrounding, we can focus on the content and make sense of it. If artworks are jammed up against one another—even great masterpieces—they look like an awful jumble best avoided. Blank space strengthens and gives value to the content within, just as rest does between the activities of our lives.

Two things I find particularly rob us of this crucial rest, of these white spaces: superfluous voices in our lives and hurry in our schedule. Both see these spaces and say, "Oh! Let me fill it!" Voices demand our attention and our decisions. Hurry pushes us into constant activity and compulsion to do and go. We must protect the white spaces. They may be empty, but they have purpose.

I've spent a good bit of time in this book telling you how to clean things physically, whether it's your body or your home. It's time for some intangible cleaning too, to make some spaces white.

DECLUTTERING THE VOICES IN OUR LIVES

When a crowd of voices populates the white spaces of my life, they drown out the ones I most want—and need—to hear: the voices of loved ones, the voices of inspiration, the voices of my own reason and imagination. These surplus voices need to go. Evicting them is not always easy, so I've identified a process:

1. **Audit the voices:** Identify the voices that speak into my day. Count in-person voices, in-print voices, voices from social media, TV, radio, podcasts, streaming, news sites, blog posts, comments, chats. My number can get into the hundreds, especially when social media is involved.

2. **Prioritize the voices:** Identify which of the above voices I most want to hear and need to hear. Make sure they get my prime time. This is so I don't get to the end of my day and realize my best atten-

tion went to voices that don't matter, that don't care, that don't even know I exist.

3. **Identify the sources of the voices and cut their access:** Log off of social media on my phone, unsubscribe from emails, turn off news notifications, block my phone's access to certain websites to make it harder for me to visit them mindlessly. Move access to a device like a desktop computer that I can't carry with me.

4. **Schedule the voices:** Voices that inspire and feed should come before voices that take. This is where rising each morning a little bit before the "have-tos" arrive can help. Take in a voice that fortifies before something arrives that depletes. We can't always control what voices are in our day, but we might control their order.

5. **Confine the voices:** Some voices, whether I like them or not, I cannot disconnect, as part of a job or other responsibility. Cushion them between positive voices, or even silence, to balance those encounters.

I regularly need to do this voice decluttering. Somehow the voices build back up over time, like clutter in a drawer.

DECLUTTERING THE HURRY FROM OUR SCHEDULE

Similarly, excess activity creates a kind of kinetic clutter around the main events of our lives, stealing their essence and their joy. When we run from one activity to the next, we rob from both. "Ruthlessly eliminate hurry from your life" is something I say to myself regularly.

I repurposed a set of questions usually applied to physical clutter:

Is it necessary in *my* life?

Does it bring *me* joy?

Very few activities are able to pass through these two gates. The emphasis I've added to *my* and *me* is crucial. Something may be necessary or joy-bringing to someone else's life, but that does not mean it is either of these for mine. We must, above all, live our own lives.

Clearing the schedule so that there were white spaces around activities brought me to a greater understanding of the idea of sabbath. So many faith traditions and self-care recommendations incorporate some idea of sabbath. A time of rest, of cessation, different from our need for sleep. It is an awake rest. A rest for the mind, heart, and spirit. As a kid, this idea would have struck me as a punishment, but as an adult, the idea is a permission and a necessity.

Michael has given this its own name in our household: Zero Time. This is time spent with zero expectations. Zero obligations. Zero musts. You do only what you choose to do. Zero Time is a grace we give ourselves from which we emerge invigorated, fed in our spirits, mentally stronger, emotionally resilient. We've regained our perspective, our purpose, and our sense of humor.

My living room is the place I most associate with Zero Time. It's a place of respite, a place to get away from hustle and hurry. A place to acknowledge that the day has held enough, and what is left undone can wait until tomorrow.

A few years ago, my oldest, the trumpet player who hadn't touched the piano in years, decided to master Beethoven's *Moonlight Sonata*—my own senior recital piece—on the piano in our living room. It was very savvy of him to pick that piece because he knew I wouldn't stop him from practicing, even if he really should have been doing other work.

As my son now plays, I remember coming home at Thanksgiving during my freshman year of college. I had just turned 18, and when I walked in the door, I was greeted by my dad playing "Happy Birthday" to me on a baby grand piano that hadn't been there when I left.

Pop was not a musical person—he didn't read music, didn't play, didn't even listen much to it. More of a talk radio guy. But he had learned, at the age of 56, to play "Happy Birthday" just for me. There was so much joy in that moment.

I still have the sign he taped on the piano that day: "For your birthday, Christmas, college graduation, marriage, and first baby shower." He lived to see all but the last one of those.

In my dad's final weeks, he would often ask me to play his favorites on the piano. "Think of Me" from *Phantom of the Opera*. Debussy's "Clair de lune." Beethoven's *Moonlight*.

My final Pop memory: it was the afternoon of my wedding. Michael and I were about to leave for our honeymoon, and my dad was lying on the sofa in the living room. He had exerted a tremendous effort to accompany me down the aisle, toast us at the reception, and dance one final "Sunrise, Sunset" with me. We knew the end was near, but we didn't realize how near.

He passed away while we were driving home six days later. This was before cell phones were common, so we did not know what awaited us. It was stunning and took me years to find the profundity in this sequence.

There has been an astonishing simultaneity of joy and sorrow in the Bronner family. It has happened far too often to be coincidental. It is God's way of reassuring us that life is a cycle, with ongoing stories that ebb and flow.

On the morning of March 7, 1997, David's child was born, the first of the next generation for my brothers and me. That same afternoon, our grandfather Dr. Emanuel Bronner passed away. The following year, my dad passed away during the week of my wedding on a day that also was his brother Ralph's birthday. In 2009, Uncle Ralph's wife, Gisela, passed away the very day their youngest grandson was born. Six years after that, Mike's son was born on our parents' anniversary, giving joy to a day that had been a reminder of what we'd lost. Death and life. Joys to distract from sorrow. Sorrows to make joys more poignant. Every generation connected to the previous.

In Celtic tradition, there are places in this world and moments in our lives where the separation between heaven and earth is just a whisper's width. They call these "thin places." In such places or at such times, the heart swells and the spirit enlivens and every breath takes in more than air. The temporal and the eternal brush shoulders. While it is impossible to remain in the thin places, it is possible to carry the memory of them, place cues to remind us of their occurrence.

The living room reminds me of such thin places, especially in the watch of the night. It is apart from the fray, where the division between the physical and the spiritual feels a little less solid. May you find such a place or come to realize you already have one. As with other rooms, this place of respite may not be your living room. It may not even be a place, but rather a time or a ritual. Wherever or whenever it is, it is where effort ceases. *Being* replaces *doing*.

I've been told to begin with the end in mind, but I am going to end with the beginning in mind. I told you earlier that I entitled my website *Going Green* to indicate an ongoing journey. That there is not a finish line and we need to reconcile with that. We must live in the "-ing."

A life thus lived is one that stewards, focuses, heals, celebrates, breathes, rests. May you find all this in the interconnectedness of soap and soul, the inner and the outer entwined. May you know life. May you know joy. May you know peace.

FIVE GENERATIONS OF SOAPMAKING

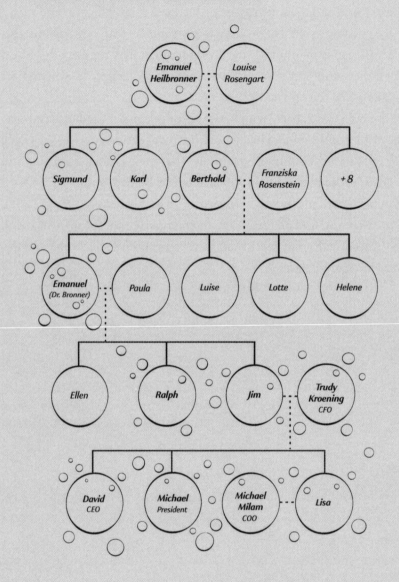

Emanuel Heilbronner first made soap in Laupheim, Germany, in 1858. His sons Sigmund, Karl, and Berthold brought the trade to Heilbronn, Germany, and my grandfather Emanuel Bronner carried it to the United States, where we still make it today. My dad, Jim, and Uncle Ralph continued the company until its transition to the current generation, where it is led by my brothers David and Mike, among others.

How Emanuel Bronner's Message of Peace Came to Be

My grandfather wrote his message long before he thought to put it on a soap label. Our family's soapmaking goes back five generations, beginning in 1858, when my grandfather's grandfather, Emanuel Heilbronner, first made soap in the basement of his home in Laupheim, Germany. Three of his sons, my great-grandfather Berthold among them, ventured off to establish their own soapmaking operation in Heilbronn, Germany, in 1903. They formed the Madaform soap company, eventually establishing three factories in the area.

My grandfather Emil, later known as Dr. Bronner, was born in 1908 in Heilbronn, the oldest and the only son. Although he was raised according to his family's Orthodox Jewish traditions, he developed a broader view of the journey of humanity. When he started sharing his thoughts in the workplace, his father, Berthold, gave him the ultimatum to nix the philosophizing or leave. My grandfather chose the latter. Based on my knowledge of him later in his life, his choice is not surprising.

He departed Hamburg on December 12, 1929, age 21. The ship's manifest records Emil Heilbronner as a 21-year-old single German male from Heilbronn who was a master soapmaker. He spent his first years in America poor but progressing. In 1933 he married a fellow German immigrant, Paula Wohlfahrt, and had three children: Ellen, Ralph, and James (my dad).

My grandfather became naturalized in 1936, at which point Emil Heilbronner took the name Emanuel Theodore Bronner. He adopted the more formal name of Emanuel, instead of the shortened version of his birth name, in honor of his grandfather, the original family soapmaker. His choice of Theodore as a middle name is a mystery to us, and later he changed it to Herbert. However, we know for certain that he dropped the Heil because of its association with Hitler.

These years in the 1930s with his young family seemed calm. My grandfather was proud and grateful for his adopted country. In a poem, he wrote:

continues

Up that flag,

Hold high the stars and stripes—

The flag of Liberty, on earth and sky it flutters.

March close together—

Descendants of all tribes;

Leave hates and jealousies down in the gutter.

Intolerance—Barbaric Ruthlessness,

Your fathers came here to fight it hell and high weather

So no matter what Hitler thinks is "best";

The pursuit of happiness is still ten times better.

The family back in Germany was facing ever-increasing restrictions as the Nazi Party moved against the Jewish people. My grandfather's sister, Luise, a chemist by training, fled to America in 1936, where she earned her doctorate and became one of the founding and first female professors at the University of Massachusetts Boston and a published poet. My grandfather's youngest sister, Lotte, fled to Palestine in 1938, living on the Ein Gev kibbutz.

However, his father, Berthold, insisted Hitler was a passing phase and refused to abandon his home. Emanuel and his sisters attempted several times to get their parents out of Germany, as in 1938, when the sisters met their parents in Switzerland for a supposed family vacation with the secret intention of escorting them on to the United States. When Berthold learned of their plan, he refused to go.

The Decree on the Exclusion of Jews from German Economic Life in 1939 required that Jewish-owned businesses be sold to Aryan owners. This included the Heilbronners' Madaform soap company, which was sold for one Deutschmark to a Dr. H. Bauder, whose letter to customers announced that the famous Madaform soap had safely passed into Aryan hands.

How Berthold, his wife, Franziska, and his widowed sister-in-law, Friederike, who lived with them, survived for the next two years we do not know, but in 1941, Berthold agreed to allow Luise to arrange emigration. Their visas to the United States arrived on December 5, 1941. Two days later, Japan bombed the United States at Pearl Harbor, and six days following, Germany declared war against the United States. Emigration was now impossible. The visas were useless.

Berthold, Franziska, and Friederike Heilbronner were arrested March 31, 1942, and deported to the Thereisienstadt concentration camp in what was then Czechoslovakia. Berthold and Friederike shortly died of illnesses brought on by the wretched conditions. Franziska survived two years at Thereisien-stadt before being sent to Auschwitz, where she was murdered in 1944.

In 1969, my Tante Luise published the following poem:

In memory of my parents who died in concentration camps
May I never forget . . .
that their light was cut off by those who do not know the source of
    all Light.
May I never forget . . .
When I see wrong done by those who judge and are not called
    upon to judge.
May I never forget . . .
When I see someone hurt by those who cannot see and by those who
    cannot hear.
May I never forget . . .
That their light was cut off but still burns in me, trying to understand,
    trying to see.

News of Emanuel's parents' demise and the war in general weighed heavily on Emanuel and Paula with their young family in Milwaukee. Paula was never strong, and she experienced a breakdown about which we have few details. She entered the Manteno State Mental Hospital in Kankakee, Illinois, where she died in 1944.

These personal tragedies, compounded with world developments, impressed upon my grandfather the conviction that humanity was on the brink of self-destruction. Further, he keenly felt the world was nearing environ-mental catastrophe, with the advent of "better living through chemistry," an

continues

ad line inspired by Dupont Chemical beginning in 1935, effectively persuading the public that nature is unpredictable and untrustworthy, and everything should be reliably synthesized in a lab.

While many in the face of such personal and global tragedies would be driven to bitterness, or at the least resignation, he launched in the opposite direction. It energized him more than ever to unify the world, to remind humanity of its commonalities, to call each individual to action wherever they find themselves.

His words were about peace and active care for ourselves, each other, and the world around us. However, with his heavy German accent, rigid posture, and emphatically clipped way of speaking—he spoke exactly as he wrote, peppered with exclamation points—he was unnerving. Furthermore, his topics did not resonate with the 1940s audience.

This reached an apex during a speech at the University of Chicago in 1946. Arrested on the charge of speaking without a permit, Emanuel was committed to the Elgin State Asylum in Illinois, where he underwent electroshock therapy.

On his third escape attempt, he succeeded and headed to California. In Los Angeles, he found a more receptive audience. Pershing Square, still to this day a hotbed for speakers with cutting-edge ideas, became his platform. In gratitude to those who came to hear him speak, he began giving away to listeners small bottles of his family's unique liquid castile soap, scented with skin-tingling peppermint essential oil, which he brewed in his tenement apartment.

Eventually he noticed that people would come for the soap and not stay to engage with the ideas. Unthwarted, he printed his ideas on the label of the soap, so that when people took the soap and inevitably were closeted in the bathroom with nothing to read, they would turn to the words on the label. A brilliant understanding of human behavior.

And thus the iconic label was born.

But what of the children? With Paula's death and Emanuel's institutionalization and escape, the children were raised in foster care in Milwaukee. Emanuel made occasional contact, but he felt that with his uncertain prospects—single, jobless, and still on the lam from a mental hospital—the children were better off in the care of others.

Regardless of the rationale, it was very hard on the children. Uncle Ralph recalls that they were in and out of 12 or more foster homes and orphanages. Eventually the three children landed with a family where they spent their teenage years. They were housed, but they were expected to work hard in the family's ballroom.

In adulthood, Uncle Ralph was philosophical about this upbringing in pointing out that "creative geniuses don't make the best fathers."[61] Uncle Ralph said he had a choice to make: to hate his father or not. He chose not to. Uncle Ralph said it was hardest on "little Jimmy"—my dad. I think my dad felt that his father had chosen his vision over his children. The only time I heard my dad lose his cool as an adult was when my grandfather tried to talk to him about the Moral ABC.

However, while Ralph and Jim eventually found their way in life, with steady careers, lifelong marriages, and three kids each, their older sister, Ellen, did not. At some point before graduating, she left high school, married briefly, and had a child named Judith, who was raised by her paternal family, with no further communication with her mother or the rest of our family. Ellen had lifelong mental and physical health issues, though we don't know a diagnosis. She spent much of her adult life hospitalized, and died in 1988. Most of this I have pieced together only recently.

Light has emerged out of Ellen's hard life. One evening in 2020, I received a message from one of my cousins that there was a woman on Ancestry.com saying she was our cousin. Her name was Judy.

And there it was. After 65 years of only questions, we finally had an answer. Ellen's daughter had been found and it has been a delight to connect with her, her children, and grandchildren.

Meanwhile, through the 1950s, while the kids remained in Milwaukee, my grandfather in Los Angeles continued delivering his message of peace with man and nature. Eventually more people wanted the soap than he could reach during his talks, so he started selling it, either directly or via small mom-and-pop health stores.

continues

When the 1960s rolled in, the audience he had always hoped for discovered him. Hippies, free thinkers, and attenders of Woodstock embraced his message and his authenticity. He had been talking love, unity, and a return to nature long before anyone was ready to hear it. Both the soap and its label soared in popularity and purchases.

At the same time his audience was increasing, his vision was declining. It had never been great, but likely was exacerbated by the electroshock therapy he underwent at Elgin. By the time I knew him, he was completely blind, but the label was firmly ensconced in his head—every word, every exclamation point. Up to the end of his eyesight, he edited and rewrote using a red crayon, which was the last implement he could see well. Then he dictated his revisions.

Dr. Bronner always felt the label was near completion and occasionally would announce triumphantly that it was finished. Until the next idea came along. The family now jokes that when he ran out of room on the label, he came up with the next scent so that he'd have more space. To this day, the different scents of the domestic Pure-Castile Liquid 16- and 32-ounce labels contain different portions of his writing.

All this time, there was no paid advertising or marketing behind the soap. It spread by word of mouth and my grandfather's indefatigable drive to converse with as many people as would listen. People told their friends about the tingly soap with the quirky label.

Word also spread via Uncle Ralph's "soap trips." Uncle Ralph became a middle school English teacher in inner-city Milwaukee. On his breaks, he'd load up his van with soap—it fit 39 cases—pick a city, and with his wife, my Aunt Gisela, visit every health store. He'd give away soap and tell the unusual story behind its label and play folk music on his ever-present acoustic guitar. You could always find Uncle Ralph by following the children who flocked to him. He was like the pied piper of soap. No one called him that, though. Instead, they called him the Opa of Soapa.

Even when the soap sold well, Dr. Bronner did not live lavishly on his profits. You would never know from the modest, unairconditioned, dimly lit one-story ranch house in which he lived and worked that he was at the helm of a successful company. He embraced a concept called Constructive Capitalism.

The idea, in his words, was to "share the profits with the workers and the earth from which you made it!" This has carried forth into business practices today as reflected in current compensation and benefits.

Even so, most of the good that the company does is built into each bottle sold. As Michael says, the greatest benefit runs through our cost of goods sold, not just in what we do with the proceeds. It's in how we source our raw materials and manufacture our products and conduct our business relationships, prioritizing organic, fair trade, and now regenerative organic practices, so that the land, the people, and the communities are all strengthened because of our work with them.

This is where our family and company story has come so far, but the next chapters are still being written. I can little imagine that Emanuel Heilbronner could have guessed what he was starting with his first batch of soap in his basement in 1858. In one way, things are coming full circle. My brothers have purchased his very house in Laupheim. The house is currently under renovation to become an assisted living home for adults with autism, who will staff a small museum in the basement to commemorate our soapmaking history.

For photographs of people mentioned, videos of Lab Coat Moments, and other supplemental material, visit SoapandSoulBook.com.

ACKNOWLEDGMENTS

Thanks to the many people who have shown me grace, especially the people I've lived with and who have seen me behind-the-scenes and have most endured the ongoingness of my journey.

Thanks to my mentors through the years—Joe Ho, Serena Whisenhunt, Elizabeth Ray, and Debbie Hamer—who have answered my questions and told me the truth.

Thanks to Patty Ladegaard, who was first my friend and then my colleague. For your editing, listening, encouraging, managing, and generally keeping everything running smoothly. Without you, this book would not be.

Thanks to Ryan Fletcher, who believed in this project unwaveringly from the beginning.

Thanks to my agent, Jud Laghi, who patiently answered all my newbie questions and guided this project smoothly through every stage.

Thanks to Sarah Ranoine, who helped me find the narrative amid the amorphous mass of my memory.

Thanks to Jay Golden of Retellable, who taught me the power of a story well-told.

Thanks to my editors, Ann Treistman and Isabel McCarthy, and the Countryman team for their enthusiasm and commitment to the vision of this book and for the innumerable ways they made it better.

Thanks to Ana Calderon, who regularly makes my spaces beautiful.

Thanks to the Boulos family of the Country Junction Deli for their hospitality in the use of their storeroom for my writing cave.

Thanks to my colleagues at Dr. Bronner's, who have answered my many questions, patiently explained scientific things to a nonscientist, answered countless "a customer wants to know" questions, and allowed me to dodge meetings and say no to projects for the past year, for your excitement and confidence.

Thanks to my mom and brothers, who let me write about our shared memories as I saw them.

Thanks to my kids, who witnessed this process on the home front, for your patience, grace, encouragement, and love.

Thanks to Michael, my soulmate, who reminds me that if I ever got my wish for everything to stop so that I could write in peace, I wouldn't have anything to write about. And who also reminds me in the midst of any mess or waywardness of life that it's all copy.

APPENDIX: INGREDIENTS TO AVOID

Eight ingredients to avoid in your personal care products:

QUATERNARY AMMONIUM COMPOUNDS (QUATS) AND UREAS: These are preservatives that release formaldehyde. Formaldehyde, while being effectively antimicrobial, is a known cause of allergic contact dermatitis, a strong sensitizer (which means it creates sensitivities over repeated exposure), and a known carcinogen.[62]

ISOTHIAZOLINONES (MESOISOTHIAZOLINONE AND METHYL-CHLOROISOTHIAZOLINONE): This is another class of preservative with high incidence of allergic contact dermatitis and sensitization.[63]

PARABENS: Specifically, propylparaben and butylparaben. These are widely used preservatives that are readily absorbed into the body and increasingly linked to endocrine disruption.[64] Parabens mimic estrogen and have been linked to reproductive, developmental, and neurological disorders; thyroid-related problems; skin allergies; and cancers.[65]

RETINYL PALMITATE: This is a form of vitamin A used in antiaging products and sunscreens. When retinyl palmitate is exposed to sunlight, it promotes the growth of skin tumors and cancer.[66] If used, use at night and wash off in the morning. Avoid in sunscreens, where it most certainly is exposed to sunlight.

POLYETHYLENE GLYCOL (PEG) AND PROPYLENE GLYCOL: These two are penetration enhancers, which means they open pathways through the skin to allow other substances to pass through.[67] This is problematic when the ingredient that passes through is considered safe for external use but not for internal. Additionally, the Centers for Disease Control (CDC) and others warn that repeated exposure to propylene glycol can produce irritation.[68] Polyethylene glycol is also ethoxylated (see next item).

ETHOXYLATED COMPOUNDS: Ethoxylated ingredients have a contamination concern. A by-product from their production is 1,4-dioxane, which is a "potential," "likely," or "reasonably anticipated" human carcinogen, depending upon which government agency you ask. Studies of products on store shelves routinely find 1,4-dioxane in a range of products that contain ethoxylated ingredients. A 2019 study found the by-product in 47 out of 82 products tested, and again in 2020, it showed up in 23 out of 39 products tested.[69] Because 1,4-dioxane is not an intentionally added ingredient and will never be listed, the best way to avoid it is to avoid ethoxylated ingredients. Ethoxylated compounds include substances containing the suffix -eth or -oxynol, Polyethylene, PEG, Polyoxyethylene, and Polysorbate.

POLY- AND PERFLOUROALKYL SUBSTANCES (PFAS): Earning their nickname "forever chemicals," PFAS are persistent, which means they don't break down, and bioaccumulative, which means they build up in the body. While the problems from PFAS are still being determined, they've already been identified as possible human carcinogens, endocrine disruptors, and immune suppressants, with further links to autoimmune diseases and reproductive disruption.[70] Their buildup in the environment is significant and enduring. While PFAS are most common in repellent surfaces—nonstick cookware, water and stain repellents on fabrics and carpets—they also show up in shampoos, makeup, and coatings on dental floss.

ETHANOLAMINES: Most problematic is diethanolamine (DEA), but related monoethanolamine (MEA) and triethanolamine (TEA) are of concern, as well. By themselves, these ethanolamine compounds are benign. However, they readily form potent carcinogens called nitrosamines when they encounter nitrogen compounds. Nitrosamines readily absorb through the skin. Such nitrogen compounds may be in other ingredients (remember the cocktail effect), or even in nitrogen oxides in the air (that's smog).[71] Even the industry's Cosmetic Ingredient Review Panel, which is notoriously reluctant to acknowledge risk, advises that ethanolamines should not be in formulations where nitroso compounds can be formed.[72] Since nitrosamines form so readily and are so readily absorbed, even in wash-off products such as shampoos, it is best to avoid these three altogether.[73]

Further Resources for Consumers

Two independent nonprofit organizations provide extensive information and guidance to consumers and have done much to advance policy for consumer and environmental safety.

ENVIRONMENTAL WORKING GROUP: Focusing on a wide range of areas from cosmetics to cleaning to water quality, the Environmental Working Group hosts two searchable databases in which consumers can look up ingredients and hazard ratings for specific products: the Skin Deep Database for cosmetics (EWG.org/skindeep) and the Guide to Healthy Cleaning for house care (EWG.org/guides/cleaners).

CAMPAIGN FOR SAFE COSMETICS: A program of Breast Cancer Prevention Partners, the Campaign for Safe Cosmetics (SafeCosmetics .org) has a wealth of guides about cosmetic safety and deeper information about ingredients.

ENDNOTES

1. Find my website and blog at LisaBronner.com.

2. California Safe Cosmetics Program (CSCP) Product Database: cscpsearch.cdph .ca.gov.

3. US Department of Agriculture, "Fact Sheet: Introduction to Organic Practices" (September 11, 2015), www.ams.usda.gov/publications/content/fact-sheet-introduction -organic-practices.

4. ZD Draelos and JC DiNardo, "A Re-Evaluation of the Comedogenicity Concept," *Journal American Academy of Dermatology* 54, no. 3 (March 2006): 507–12. https://doi .org/10.1016/j.jaad.2005.11.1058.

5. A Steinemann, "Volatile Emissions from Common Consumer Products," *Air Quality, Atmosphere & Health* 8 (2015): 273–281. https://doi.org/10.1007/s11869-015-0327-6.

6. J O'Doherty et al., "Beauty in a Smile: The Role of Medial Orbitofrontal Cortex in Facial Attractiveness," *Neuropsychologia* 41, no. 2 (2003): 147–55. https://doi.org/10 .1016/s0028-3932(02)00145-8; NC Hass, TD Weston, and S-L Lim, "Be Happy Not Sad for Your Youth: The Effect of Emotional Expression on Age Perception," *PLoS ONE* 11, no. 3 (2016): e0152093. https://doi.org/10.1371/journal.pone.0152093; TD Weston, NC Hass, and S-L Lim, "The Effect of Sad Facial Expressions on Weight Judgment," *Frontiers in Psychology* 6 (April 10, 2015). https://doi.org/10.3389/fpsyg.2015.00417.

7. US Food and Drug Administration, "Allergens in Cosmetics" (February 25, 2022), www.fda.gov/cosmetics/cosmetic-ingredients/allergens-cosmetics.

8. AR Vaughn et al., "Natural Oils for Skin-Barrier Repair: Ancient Compounds Now Backed by Modern Science," *American Journal of Clinical Dermatology* 19, no. 1 (February 2018):103–117. https://doi.org/10.1007/s40257-017-0301-1.

9. N Poljšak, S Kreft, and N Kočevar Glavač, "Vegetable Butters and Oils in Skin Wound Healing: Scientific Evidence for New Opportunities in Dermatology," *Phytotherapy Research* 34, no. 2 (February 2020): 254–269. https://doi.org/10.1002/ptr.6524.

10. V Mikulcová et al., "Formulation, Characterization, and Properties of Hemp Seed Oil and Its Emulsions," *Molecules* 22, no. 5 (April 27, 2017): 700. https://doi.org/10.3390 /molecules22050700; S Metwally et al., "PCL Patches with Controlled Fiber Morphology

and Mechanical Performance for Skin Moisturization via Long-Term Release of Hemp Oil for Atopic Dermatitis," *Membranes* (Basel) 11, no. 1 (December 31, 2020): 26. https://doi.org/10.3390/membranes11010026.

11. C Hess, M Krämer, and B Madea, "Topical Application of THC Containing Products Is Not Able to Cause Positive Cannabinoid Finding in Blood or Urine," *Forensic Science International* 272 (March 2017): 68–71. https://doi.org/10.1016/j.forsciint.2017.01.008.

12. K Khanpara, JV Renuka, and C Harisha, "A Detailed Investigation on Shikakai (*Acacia Concinna Linn.*) Fruit," *Journal of Current Pharmaceutical Research* 99 (January 2021): 6–10. www.researchgate.net/publication/280313608_A_detailed_investigation_on_shikakai_Acacia_concinna_Linn_fruit.

13. SA Ventura and GB Kasting, "Dynamics of Glycerine and Water Transport across Human Skin from Binary Mixtures," *International Journal of Cosmetic Science* 39 (April 2017):165–78. https://doi.org/10.1111/ics.12362; B Burlando and L Cornara, "Honey in Dermatology and Skin Care: A Review," *Journal of Cosmetic Dermatology* 12, no. 4 (December 2013): 306–313. https://doi.org/10.1111/jocd.12058.

14. L Chularojanamontri et al., "Moisturizers for Acne: What Are Their Constituents?" *The Journal of Clinical and Aesthetic Dermatology* 7 no. 5 (May 2014): 36–44.

15. D Khnykin et al., "Role of Fatty Acid Transporters in Epidermis: Implications for Health and Disease." *Dermato-Endocrinology* 3, no. 2 (2011): 53–61. https://doi.org/10.4161/derm.3.2.14816; S Purnamawati et al., "The Role of Moisturizers in Addressing Various Kinds of Dermatitis: A Review," *Clinical Medicine & Research* 15, no. 3–4 (December 1, 2017): 75–87. https://doi.org/10.3121/cmr.2017.1363.

16. WE Morris, E William, and SC Kwan, "Use of the Rabbit Ear Model in Evaluating the Comedogenic Potential of Cosmetic Ingredients," *Journal of the Society of Cosmetic Chemists* 34 (1983): 215–25.

17. SB Frank, "Is the Rabbit Ear Model, in Its Present State, Prophetic of Acnegenicity?" *Journal of the American Academy of Dermatology* 6, no. 3 (March 1982): 373–77. https://doi.org/10.1016/S0190-9622(82)70032-5.

18. Draelos, "A Re-Evaluation of Comedogenicity," 507–12.

19. American Academy of Dermatology Association, "Caring for Tattooed Skin," (accessed June 13, 2022), www.aad.org/public/everyday-care/skin-care-basics/tattoos/caring-for-tattooed-skin.

20. P Sharma, S Garg, and NM Kalra, "Effect of Denture Cleansers on Surface Roughness and Flexural Strength of Heat Cure Denture Base Resin: An In Vitro Study," *Journal of Clinical and Diagnostic Research* 11, no. 8 (August 2017): ZC94–ZC97. https://doi.org/10.7860/JCDR/2017/27307.10483.

21. F Keyf and T Güngör, "Comparison of Effects of Bleach and Cleansing Tablet on Reflectance and Surface Changes of a Dental Alloy Used for Removable Partial Dentures," *Journal of Biomaterials Applications* 18, no. 1 (July 2003): 5–14. https://doi.org/10.1177/0885328203018001001.

22. DD Gummin et al., "2020 Annual Report of the American Association of Poison Control Centers' National Poison Data System (NPDS): 38th Annual Report," *Clinical Toxicology* 59, no. 12 (2021): 1282–1501. https://doi.org/10.1080/15563650.2021.1989785.

23. N Nematollahi et al., "Volatile Chemical Emissions from Fragranced Baby Products," *Air Quality, Atmosphere & Health* 11, no. 7 (2018): 785–90. https://doi.org/10.1007/s11869 -018-0593-1; RE Dodson et al., "Endocrine Disruptors and Asthma-Associated Chemicals in Consumer Products," *Environmental Health Perspectives* 120, no. 7 (2012): 935–43. https://doi.org/10.1289/ehp.1104052; S Sathyanarayana et al., "Baby Care Products: Possible Sources of Infant Phthalate Exposure," *Pediatrics* 121, no. 2 (February 2008): e260–8. https://doi.org/10.1542/peds.2006-3766; Y Guo and K Kannan, "A Survey of Phthalates and Parabens in Personal Care Products from the United States and its Implications for Human Exposure," *Environmental Science & Technology* 47, no. 24 (2013): 14442–9. https://doi .org/10.1021/es4042034; W Zhou, "The Determination of 1,4-Dioxane in Cosmetic Products by Gas Chromatography with Tandem Mass Spectrometry," *Journal of Chromatography A* 1607 (December 6, 2019): 460400. https://doi.org/10.1016/j.chroma.2019.460400.

24. JS Lund and M Feldt-Rasmussen, "Accidental Aspiration of Talc," *Acta Pædiatrica* 58, no. 3 (May 1969): 295–96. https://doi.org/10.1111/j.1651-2227.1969.tb04721.x; P Silver et al., "Respiratory Failure from Corn Starch Aspiration: A Hazard of Diaper Changing," *Pediatric Emergency Care* 12, no. 2 (April 1996): 108–10. https://doi.org/10.1097/00006565 -199604000-00011.

25. US Food and Drug Administration, "How Safe Are Color Additives?" (August 3, 2021), www.fda.gov/consumers/consumer-updates/how-safe-are-color-additives.

26. N Latorre, JF Silvestre, and AF Monteagudo, "Dermatitis de contacto alérgica por formaldehído y liberadores de formaldehído [Allergic Contact Dermatitis Caused by Formaldehyde and Formaldehyde Releasers]," *Actas Dermosifiliogr* 102, no. 2 (March 2011): 86–97. Spanish. https://doi.org/10.1016/j.ad.2010.09.004.

27. US Food and Drug Administration, "1,4-Dioxane in Cosmetics: A Manufacturing Byproduct" (August 3, 2022), https://www.fda.gov/cosmetics/potential-contaminants -cosmetics/14-dioxane-cosmetics-manufacturing-byproduct.

28. A Haq and B Michniak-Kohn, "Effects of Solvents and Penetration Enhancers on Transdermal Delivery of Thymoquinone: Permeability and Skin Deposition Study," *Drug Delivery* 25, no. 1 (November 2018):1943–49. https://doi.org/10.1080/10717544 .2018.1523256; US Department of Health and Human Services, Public Health Service, "Toxicological profile for Propylene Glycol," Agency for Toxic Substances and Disease Registry (1997), wwwn.cdc.gov/TSP/PHS/PHS.aspx?phsid=1120&toxid=240 .

29. AK Rush et al., "Eliminating Cocamidopropyl Betaine–Induced Allergic Contact Dermatitis: A New Benign-by-Design Zwitterionic Surfactant," *Journal of the American Academy of Dermatology* 79, no. 3 (September 2018): AB127. https://doi.org/10.1016/j .jaad.2018.05.532.

30. MK Matta et al., "Effect of Sunscreen Application on Plasma Concentration of Sunscreen Active Ingredients: A Randomized Clinical Trial, " *JAMA* 323, no. 3 (2020): 256–67. https://doi.org/10.1001/jama.2019.20747.

31. US Food and Drug Administration, "Questions and Answers: FDA Posts Deemed Final Order and Proposed Order for Over-the-Counter Sunscreen" (September 24, 2021), www.fda.gov/drugs/understanding-over-counter-medicines/questions-and-answers-fda -posts-deemed-final order and proposed order over-counter-sunscreen.

32. J Hawkins et al., "Prevalence of Endocrine Disorders among Children Exposed to Lavender Essential Oil and Tea Tree Essential Oils," *International Journal of Pediatrics & Adolescent Medicine* 9, no. 2 (2022): 117–24. https://doi.org/10.1016/j.ijpam.2021.10.001.

33. ES Kurtz and W Wallo, "Colloidal Oatmeal: History, Chemistry and Clinical Properties," *Journal of Drugs in Dermatology* 6, no. 2 (2007): 167–70.

34. See LisaBronner.com.

35. Center for Disease Control and Prevention, "When and How to Clean and Disinfect Your Home" (February 23, 2023), www.cdc.gov/hygiene/cleaning/cleaning-your-home.html.

36. J Qi et al., "Evaluation of the Antibacterial Effect of Tea Tree Oil on Enterococcus Faecalis and Biofilm in Vitro," *Journal of Ethnopharmacology* 281 (December 5, 2021): 114566. https://doi.org/10.1016/j.jep.2021.114566.

37. A Fahimipour et al., "Daylight Exposure Modulates Bacterial Communities Associated with Household Dust," *Microbiome* 6 (2018): 175. https://doi.org/10.1186/s40168-018-0559-4.

38. Environmental Protection Agency, "Indoor Air Quality" (September 1, 2021), www.epa.gov/report-environment/indoor-air-quality.

39. World Health Organization, "Antimicrobial Resistance" (November 17, 2021), www.who.int/news-room/fact-sheets/detail/antimicrobial-resistance.

40. M Kim et al., "Widely Used Benzalkonium Chloride Disinfectants Can Promote Antibiotic Resistance," *Applied and Environmental Microbiology* 84, no. 17 (August 17, 2018): e01201–18. https://doi.org/10.1128/AEM.01201-18.

41. G Kampf. "Acquired Resistance to Chlorhexidine—Is It Time to Establish an 'Antiseptic Stewardship' Initiative?" *The Journal of Hospital Infection* 94, no. 3 (2016): 213–27. https://doi.org/10.1016/j.jhin.2016.08.018/.

42. E Heir et al., "Kan desinfeksjonsmidler bidra til bakteriell antibiotikaresistens? [Can Disinfectants Contribute to Antibiotic Resistance?]," *Tidsskrift for den Norske laegeforening : tidsskrift for praktisk medicin, ny raekke* 121, no. 27 (2001): 3201–6.

43. LG McDonald and E Tovey., "The Role of Water Temperature and Laundry Procedures in Reducing House Dust Mite Populations and Allergen Content of Bedding," *The Journal of Allergy and Clinical Mmmunology* 90, no. 4, pt. 1 (October 1992): 599–608. https://doi.org/10.1016/0091-6749(92)90132-l.

44. H Rae, "Here's Why New Appliances Use Less Energy." *Consumer Reports* (April 21, 2019), www.consumerreports.org/energy-efficiency/why-new-major-appliances-use-less-energy.

45. K Laitala, C Boks , and IG Klepp, "Potential for Environmental Improvements in Laundering," *International Journal of Consumer Studies* 35 (2011): 254–264. https://doi.org/10.1111/j.1470-6431.2010.00968.x.

46. A Steinemann, "Fragranced Consumer Products: Exposures and Effects from Emissions," *Air Quality, Atmosphere & Health* 9, no. 8 (2016): 861–66. https://doi.org/10.1007/s11869-016-0442-z.

47. RC Anderson and JH Anderson, "Respiratory Toxicity of Fabric Softener Emissions," *Journal of Toxicology and Environmental Health, Part A* 60, no. 2 (2000): 121–36. https://doi.org/10.1080/009841000156538.

48. MJ Reeder, "Allergic Contact Dermatitis to Fragrances," *Dermatologic Clinics* 38, no. 3 (2020): 371–77. https://doi.org/10.1016/j.det.2020.02.009.

49. K Mikio et al., "Hazard Evaluation of Household Detergents, Fabric Softeners, Shampoos and Conditioners by Acute Immobilization Test Using Daphnia magna," *Journal of Japan Society on Water Environment* 27 (2004): 741–46. https://doi.org/10.2965/jswe.27.741.

50. GC Steinhardt and CJ Egler, "Keep the 'Dirty Dozen' Out of Your Onsite Sewage System (Septic Tank)," *Home & Environment*, Purdue University College of the Environment, (April 2018), https://www.extension.purdue.edu/extmedia/HENV/HENV -106-W.pdf.

51. California Air Resources Board, "Phase Out of Perchloroethylene from the Dry Cleaning Process" (accessed April 25, 2022), ww2.arb.ca.gov/our-work/programs/phase -out-perchloroethylene-dry-cleaning-process.

52. Center for Disease Control and Prevention, "Control of Exposure to Perchloroethylene in Commercial Drycleaning (Substitution)," The National Institute for Occupational Safety and Health (June 6, 2014), www.cdc.gov/niosh/docs/hazardcontrol/hc17 .html.

53. M Richold, "Boron Exposure from Consumer Products," *Biological Trace Element Research* 66, no. 1–3 (1998): 121–9. https://doi.org/10.1007/BF02783132.

54. Y Duydu et al., "Reproductive Toxicity Parameters and Biological Monitoring in Occupationally and Environmentally Boron-Exposed Persons in Bandirma, Turkey," *Archives of Toxicology* 85, no. 6 (2011): 589–600. https://doi.org/10.1007/s00204-011 -0692-3.

55. GC Steinhardt, "Keep the 'Dirty Dozen' Out."

56. AM Helmenstine, "Corrosive Definition in Chemistry," *ThoughtCo.* (November 10, 2019), www.thoughtco.com/definition-of-corrosive-604961.

57. C Kratzer, "Selection and Use of Home Cleaning Products," New Mexico State University Cooperative Extension Service College of Agriculture and Home Economics (May 2008), https://cannon.tennessee.edu/wp-content/uploads/sites/85/2020/04/4H -Judging-CDM-Study-Cleaning-Products.pdf.

58. EA Bannan and LF Judge, "Bacteriological Studies Relating to Handwashing," American Journal of Public Health and the Nations Health 55, no. 6 (June 1965): 915–22. https:// doi.org/10.2105/ajph.55.6.915; JE Heinze and F Yackovich, "Washing with Contaminated Bar Soap Is Unlikely to Transfer Bacteria," *Epidemiology & Infection* 101, no. 1 (August 1988): 135–42. https://doi.org/10.1017/s0950268800029290.

59. L Xu et al., "Molecular Mechanisms Underlying Menthol Binding and Activation of TRPM8 Ion Channel," *Nature Communications* 11 (2020): 3790. https://doi.org/10 .1038/s41467-020-17582-x.

60. HK Malhi et al., "Tea Tree Oil Gel for Mild to Moderate Acne: A 12 Week Uncontrolled, Open-Label Phase II Pilot Study," *Australasian Journal of Dermatology* 58, no. 3 (August 2017): 205–210. https://doi.org/10.1111/ajd.12465; LO Felipe et al., "Lactoferrin, Chitosan and Melaleuca alternifolia—Natural Products that Show Promise in Candidi-

asis Treatment," *Brazilian Journal of Microbiology* 49, no. 2 (April–June 2018): 212–19. https://doi.org/10.1016/j.bjm.2017.05.008; J Sharifi-Rad et al., "Plants of the Melaleuca Genus as Antimicrobial Agents: From Farm to Pharmacy," *Phytotherapy Research* 31, no. 10 (October 2017): 1475–94. https://doi.org/10.1002/ptr.5880.

61. M Snyder, "Dr. Bronner Attempts to Save the World with Soap," *OnMilwaukee* (October 26, 2006), https://onmilwaukee.com/articles/drbronnersoap.

62. A de Groot et al., "Formaldehyde-Releasers in Cosmetics: Relationship to Formaldehyde Contact Allergy," *Contact Dermatitis* 62, no. 1 (January 2010): 18–31. https://doi.org/10.1111/j.1600-0536.2009.01631.x.

63. B Kręcisz, D Chomiczewska-Skóra, and M Kieć-Świerczyńska, "Konserwanty jako istotne czynniki etiologiczne alergicznego kontaktowego zapalenia skóry [Preservatives as important etiologic factors of allergic contact dermatitis]," *Medycyna Pracy* 66, no. 3 (2015): 327–32. Polish. https://doi.org/10.13075/mp.5893.00176.

64. J Boberg et al., "Possible Endocrine Disrupting Effects of Parabens and Their Metabolites," *Reproductive Toxicology* 30, no. 2 (September 2010): 301–12. https://doi.org/10.1016/j.reprotox.2010.03.011.

65. P Mitra et al., "An Overview of Endocrine Disrupting Chemical Paraben and Search for an Alternative–A Review," *Proceedings of the Zoological Society* 74 (2021): 479–93. https://doi.org/10.1007/s12595-021-00418-x.

66. National Toxicology Program, "Photocarcinogenesis Study of Retinoic Acid and Retinyl Palmitate [CAS Nos. 302-79-4 (All-trans-retinoic acid) and 79-81-2 (All-trans-retinyl palmitate)] in SKH-1 Mice (Simulated Solar Light and Topical Application Study)," *National Toxicology Program Technical Report Series* 586 (July 2012): 1–352. PMID: 23001333.

67. MD Boudreau et al., "Photo-co-carcinogenesis of Topically Applied Retinyl Palmitate in SKH-1 Hairless Mice," *Photochemistry and Photobiology* 93, no. 4 (July 2017): 1096–1114. https://doi.org/10.1111/php.12730.

68. Center for Disease Control and Prevention, "Toxicological Profile for Propylene Glycol," Agency for Toxic Substances and Disease Registry (March 25, 2014), www.cdc.gov/TSP/ToxProfiles/ToxProfiles.aspx?id=1122&tid=240.

69. W Zhou, "The Determination of 1,4-Dioxane in Cosmetic Products." IH Alsohaimi et al., "Solvent Extraction and Gas Chromatography-Mass Spectrometric Determination of Probable Carcinogen 1,4-Dioxane in Cosmetic Products," *Scientific Reports* 23, no. 10 (March 23, 2020): 5214. https://doi.org/10.1038/s41598-020-62149-x.

70. National Cancer Institute, "PFAS Exposure and Risk of Cancer," Division of Cancer Epidemiology & Genetics, https://dceg.cancer.gov/research/what-we-study/pfas; MJ Lopez-Espinosa et al., "Thyroid Function and Perfluoroalkyl Acids in Children Living Near a Chemical Plant," *Environmental Health Perspectives* 120 (2012): 1036–41. https://doi.org/10.1289/ehp.1104370.

71. G Eisenbrand, A Fuchs, and W Koehl, "N-nitroso Compounds in Cosmetics, Household Commodities and Cutting Fluids," *European Journal of Cancer Prevention* 5 (September 1996): 41–46.

72. MM Fiume et al., "Safety Assessment of Diethanolamine and Its Salts as Used in Cosmetics," *International Journal of Toxicol*ogy 36, no. 5 (September/October 2017): 89S–110S. https://doi.org/10.1177/1091581817707179.

73. TJ Franz et al., "Percutaneous Penetration of N-nitrosodiethanolamine through Human Skin (in Vitro): Comparison of Finite and Infinite Dose Applications from Cosmetic Vehicles," *Fundamental and Applied Toxicology* 21, no. 2 (August 1993): 213–21. https://doi.org/10.1006/faat.1993.1091.

INDEX